FROM

HURT

— TO —

HEALING

FROM

HURT

— TO —

HEALING

**ALLOWING GOD'S MERCY TO TRIUMPH
OVER HURT FROM THE CHURCH**

*May God's Blessings Overtake you,
His Love Overwhelm you and His
Peace surround you !*

Mandy B. Pierce

MANDY B PIERCE

XULON PRESS

Xulon Press
2301 Lucien Way #415
Maitland, FL 32751
407.339.4217
www.xulonpress.com

Unless otherwise indicated, Scripture quotations taken from the New King James Version (NKJV). Copyright © 1982 by Thomas Nelson, Inc. Used by permission. All rights reserved.

Scripture quotations taken from the Holy Bible, New Living Translation (NLT). Copyright ©1996, 2004, 2007 by Tyndale House Foundation. Used by permission of Tyndale House Publishers, Inc.

Address all personal correspondence to:

Mandybpierce.com

Individuals and church groups may order books from website directly or from the publisher. Retailers and wholesalers should order from our distributors. Refer to the Xulon Press website for distribution information.

Printed in the United States of America.

ISBN-13: 978-1-5456-7871-8

DEDICATION

~✎ ✎~

To my husband Tom, thank you for allowing me the many hours it takes in prayer and staying before God while writing. You are the best and most godly husband a gal could possibly ask for. To my sons, T.J. and Caleb, you are such blessings in my life. I rejoice as I watch you and your beautiful wives, Katie (T.J.s wife) and Ali (Caleb's wife), aka my daughters-in-love, walking the path of purpose and promise God has specifically designed for you. I pray Jeremiah 29:11 explodes within your lives and launches you into your destinies.

To my friend Tina, over many years you remained my biggest fan in whatever I had written, large or small. The question you asked as you were going through the toughest battle of your life was the inspiration for this book. I praise God for our many years of friendship and all I saw Christ do in and through your life. I know you are now rooting me on from the courts of Heaven, and I love you for it. You will always remain my biggest fan!

To my mother, who imparted into my life so many things, among which was her love for writing, and for always being there throughout my life. Thanks, Mom! To my father, who became a changed man in Christ, thank you for not just telling us to love God but showing by your life's example also. I know you are now in that cloud of witnesses cheering me on as I step into that which has been my life's passion. Thanks, Pops!

And to all my friends and family who have "kept the faith" and prayed for me the many years this book has been written, awaiting the day my courage and faith would collide, thank you! Today is that day—praise the Lord!

Lastly, to Pastor Sandra Roach and Ms. Margie Newsom, my heart melts with gratitude for the time you spent leading me through the process of inner healing. I know it wasn't easy, but you refused to give up, and I am forever grateful. You two are, without question, "The Dynamic Duo!"

CONTENTS

❧ ❧

DEDICATION. v

FOREWORD ix

ACKNOWLEDGEMENT xi

INTRODUCTION. xiii

Chapter 1   THE QUESTION WAS ASKED. 1

Chapter 2   QUESTION ANSWERED 19

Chapter 3   SO, WHO AM I? 52

Chapter 4   OUR HEAVENLY DNA 78

Chapter 5   RISE TO THE CALL 97

Chapter 6   GO! WITH CARE 114

Chapter 7   ENTER IN. 132

FOREWORD

꙳

The Apostle Paul wrote of the Church, saying Jesus would *"present her to Himself a glorious church, not having spot or wrinkle or any such thing, but that she would be holy and without blemish"* (Eph. 5:27).

More and more people are leaving the church because of hurt inflicted within the family of God. Many of those carrying the scars of repeated abuse never return. Mandy Pierce allows her readers to walk through her journey from *hurt to healing*.

Contained within the pages of this book, you will see God's grace unfold in the life of a woman who had given up on the church. In the midst of her wilderness, she had an encounter with God that would begin her pathway to healing.

It is Mandy's heart to see the church healed and living out its purpose in these last days. I pray that you will find your own path back to the heart of God as you read this book.

Sandra Roach
Lead Pastor, *Summit Church-Pigeon Forge*

ACKNOWLEDGEMENT

~≈ ≈~

I will never forget approaching my pastor in January 2009.

"Pastor, I have written a book and feel led to ask if you would consider reviewing it to see if there is hope for publication." I nervously awaited her answer with no clue of how she might respond. I had only been at this church a few weeks, so she hardly even knew my name. Yes, it was an extremely odd thing to ask of someone I'd known for such a short period of time, yet I knew it was a "God-thing." Had this pastor known me long, she too would have known this was *totally* out of my character. There had to be something, or *Someone*, giving me this boldness.

Graciously, my invitation was accepted, and the following week, I placed the manuscript in her hands. From that moment on, what took place was a journey of walking together for more than a year. What had begun merely as a testimony of what God *did*, has now become a living work of who He is and who we are in Him.

As we met weekly, walking through the pages of this book, the Holy Spirit met with us and brought forth glorious revelation. He placed His *super* on our *natural* and penned what only He could.

I must give credit where it is due and acknowledge Sandra Wilson Roach for her many contributions, steadfastness, and prayer poured into this book and over my life. Thank you for being that woman of God who walks beside her sheep, guiding, encouraging, and strengthening them as they are launched by the hand of God into their destinies. Thank you for the selfless hours spent in prayer and unending days dedicated to the Body of Christ. Being a woman pastor is by far not an easy call, yet you stand boldly, love loudly and press on toward the mark of His high calling.

I can never fully express my love and gratitude for all you imparted into my life over the ten-year period as my pastor and continue to impart into my life as my spiritual mom. It was when I felt I was at the "end" of life's rope, never to be used by God again, that I was lovingly placed by Him into your care. I now see through His love and faithfulness, what I thought the end was merely a new beginning in Christ. Thank you for helping me to understand my true Identity!

Much thanks and much love . . .

From the depths of my heart.

INTRODUCTION

~≈ ≈~

I have been in church all my life. I've seen "the Church" through the eyes of a child as well as through the eyes of a hurt, angry, and bitter woman. I've walked with believers who I thought would be a part of my life for as long as breath remained within us, and I've picked myself up after the dagger was plunged from behind. So often I would question if it was even worth the effort to "dress her up and take her" to church. After all, what's the point?

But one glorious day, after all the pain I'd endured and years spent in and out of people's lives, I encountered the answer to my "why's."

I'd been a Christian for many years but had no depth in my understanding of the importance of God's House or His people. I loved the Lord but did not understand His love living through me. And you see, until God's love is a living spring flowing out of you and spilling into the lives of others, you'll never know how to go beyond hurt to live in healing—to live in what God's Word calls zoë. In the Gospel of John, Jesus is recorded as saying "...I have come that they may have life, and that they may have it more abundantly" (John 10:10). The word *life* in this verse, is translated from the original Greek word *zoë*. Zoë is one of several Greek words used in the New Testament that mean life (Bible Study Tools, 2019). We know that this life that Jesus describes is not just a walking, talking, and breathing life. This zoë life is an abundant life filled with vitality and promise. This zoë life is a life that is not only real and genuine and devoted to God, but it is also a life that is overflowing with more blessings than we deserve.

Why did David proclaim in Psalm 122:1, "I was glad when they said to me, Let us go into the house of the Lord"? He had to know something the Church today is missing.

Why does the Bible admonish us in Hebrews 10:25, "not forsaking the assembling of ourselves together, as is the manner of some, but exhorting one another, and so much the more as you see the Day approaching"? Why bother when the Church is full of hypocrites, backbiters, and gossipers?

I've crossed this river of "why's" and journeyed through hell and back in my quest of seeking answers. Many today have been so hurt by the Church, they have vowed never to return there. Some have even turned their backs on God, blaming Him for their mistreatment. Oh, my precious brothers and sisters, we have gotten it so wrong. The enemy has laughed for such a long period of time, thinking the wedge driven between believers and God's House is irreparable. But hell forgot one important attribute – God's House is no longer made of wood and stone. We are the living stones of His temple – Jesus lives through His children!

Introduction

Every child of God has a call on their life and a bullseye on their back. If it is possible for the enemy of their soul to penetrate that shield with a lie so subtle they never know it's coming, then perhaps the damage will be so devastating it will keep them from ever stepping into the fullness of joy God designed for their life. That, my friend, is what hurt in the Church was designed to do – keep you from the very destiny God designed specifically for you.

But how do you overcome the damage that's been done? How could *anyone* possibly understand what you have endured? And is it possible to merely move on as though everything is okay?

Yes, a thousand times yes! There is not only a way to move beyond, but a place of victory that awaits you. God's House was never intended to be a place of hurt, but rather a house of healing. And He is there even now, waiting for you to return. We must never allow life to keep us from divine destiny.

From the time I was a little girl, hell sought to cripple me with wounds of bitterness and rejection. This pain carried on into my adult life and my walk with God. Why did this happen? Because the enemy knows if he can get you in that position, he can render you powerless. And sadly enough, there are victims of his ploy who leave this world having never known they were victors.

Walk with me through the pages of this book. See a life held captive by lies, and experience the explosion of God's transforming power. Then look into the lens of your life and understand God desires to do the very same for you.

The struggle can be over. God has so much destined for you. Determine that today is the day you overcome hurt, gain understanding, and step into the fullness of who you are. That position hell rendered you powerless in will now be the seat from which you reign victorious, as you journey from hurt to healing!

≈ Chapter 1 ≈

THE
QUESTION WAS ASKED

S omeone approached me asking, "How would you define a Christian?"

"Why?" I asked. "Is someone disclaiming your theology?"

"No. I guess I just have a lot of unanswered questions in my life, and lately, I wonder if I really am one. All I want is a brief definition. So please tell me in simple terms how you would define a Christian."

"Well," I began, "a Christian, simply put, is someone who has… a Christian is one who knows… a Christian is…"

I sat in silence. Had I been asked this question a few years earlier, I could have answered without hesitation. I would have answered with harsh frankness and absolutely no regard for feelings or convictions of others. For then, I was highly intelligent. It was remarkable. I would watch people and listen to them for a while, and I knew (even better than they) who was *really* a Christian and who was not. I judged others at work, in church, my neighbors, and even close friends. "She's awesome," I'd say. "If ever anyone

1

is glory-bound, it's Bridget. She is always working for the Lord. Now, Lori, I still question. She says she loves the Lord, but I doubt she really even knows Him."

Yes sir, I was an expert on the life of a Christian. I'd question those belonging to denominational churches whose doctrine I may not understand or perhaps not totally agree on. If anyone dared to question *my* faith or *my* relationship with the Lord – or their relationship with the Lord – I had a definite answer ready. Bring it on! If you were in doubt, I would figure it out, because I pretty much knew who was going to Heaven and who was bound for the pit of hell.

I knew precisely, unequivocally, and without question what a Christian really was. That is, until my world fell apart and sent my entire life into a tailspin.

❧ ❧

Where shall I begin?

Have you heard the old cliché, "the best place to start is at the beginning"? Let's do! If you are going to tell a story, you must have a firm foundation on which to build. We all learned from our childhood Bible stories what happens when you build upon shaky ground. Jesus taught in Matthew 7:26-27 of the builder who built his house upon the sand. I must admit, I've built a few of those "sandcastles" in my day too; beautiful and seemingly solid, until the first storm passes through. It is in the passing of the storm and washing of the waters (a tsunami sometimes) that your foundation either remains solid, though shaken, or as the Bible so clearly states in the parable, it falls, and great is the fall.

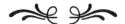

It is in the passing of the storm and washing of the waters (a tsunami sometimes) that your foundation either remains solid, though shaken, or as the Bible so clearly states in the parable, it falls, and great is the fall.

Let's begin -

Things were a little tough as a tot. I vaguely remember the age of three. The story that most vividly comes to mind was my little Suzy doll. She was my baby. She slept with me, ate with me (well, she took her pretend bottle while I, "the big girl," ate from a plate), and anytime reassurance was needed, there she was. I could always depend on Suzy. That is, until the day an *outsider* came calling.

It was terribly traumatic. I don't recall exactly how I started missing Suzy, but I do remember running through the yard yelling her name. "Thuzy, Thuzy doll. Mere to your mommy, Thuzy." As I ran into the side yard, my mother and brother came toward me. Their faces said it all.

"Where my Thuzy doll?" As I asked, my mother looked as though she was deep in thought. With hands behind her back, she began to kneel in front of me and bring her arms around in a motion that indicated a hug was sure to be needed. All at once my brother screamed, "Your stupid Suzy doll got ate – LOOK!" As his hand swung around, there was my precious Suzy doll's head–in his hand.

I burst into tears, more like deep sobbing. What heart-break! What trauma! How on earth would I make it through the death of Suzy? We had family pictures with her by my side. Her locks of gold (really it was synthetic hair that was literally matted and tangled together where I never combed it, just licked it and smoothed it out now and then). Her little perfect body (well the arms, legs and face felt real, the rest of her torso was just stuffing wrapped in a small burlap-type body). But regardless of how others saw her, she was *my* Suzy. As a three-year-old that day, in the side yard of our little family home, in a neighborhood nestled at the outskirts of the city of Knoxville, Tennessee, I knew things could never, ever possibly get any worse . . .

Time went on; I became older and more aware of my sur-roundings. I realized much more about how home-life operated too. My mother was always helping my two older brothers with homework while dinner would cook in the oven. I would watch *The New Zoo Revue* and the *Electric Company*, soaking in all I could to learn my sounds and numbers, hoping to one day be as smart as them.

The other thing I remember most about that early age was what happened every evening as the sun began to set. I would run to the window to look out. Reaching the windowsill, I would close my eyes and then open them little by little as I glared toward the driveway. My heart would pound as though it were going to explode in my chest, and I would whisper, "Please God, don't let Daddy be home." When my eyes opened to an empty driveway, I would let out a sweet sigh of relief and run back to my crayons or whatever I was doing before noticing the dusk.

Sometimes one of my brothers would see me running to the window, and they'd jump up, "Is it Daddy? Is it? Well, answer." They didn't understand, I had a pattern to follow, and it took a little time. I couldn't just rush to the window with eyes wide open. If *he* happened to be there, it would be way too traumatic to handle without first preparing myself.

On those days, I would answer "No. The coast is clear." My brother would then say, "Good. I hope he never comes home again."

Mom listened and knew perfectly well why we felt the way we did. All of us, including her, feared Daddy. Later in life, Mom explained what led to Dad's drunkenness, and I understood the battle he fought. As a child living in the home of an alcoholic, I must tell you however, it was not fun. No one, absolutely no one, understands how it feels unless they have been there.

On those evenings Dad did not come home, Mom would go about her business of cooking dinner, feeding us, finishing up homework, and making sure we all had our baths. She would then gather us around the coffee table in the living room. "It doesn't look like Daddy will make it home tonight. We need to pray for him and ask Jesus to keep him safe and help him find his way home. Most importantly, we need to ask Jesus to save Daddy's soul. Daddy needs Jesus to come and live in his heart."

I remember one night while going through this routine, it just spilled out, the true feelings of a child trying to understand why Daddy acted this way. Why, when he did come home, my brothers and I had to lock ourselves in the bedroom with an outside door while my oldest brother ran to the neighbor's house for help. Why Daddy was so mean that my other brother and I would literally fling our bodies against the interior bedroom door, screaming for him to stop as we'd hear things flying across the living room – furniture, tables, and on a few occasions it was our mother who received the brunt of his drunken stupor. Why we had to listen at those times he'd come to the bedroom door hollering, "You stupid kids better shut your mouths or you're next. I MEAN IT!" As he would hit his fist against the door, the agony of thinking this would surely be the time he really knocked the door down and beat us to death. My brother would shout, "Come on, push on the door. Don't let it open, he'll kill us. Push!" I'd be crying so hard I could barely even stand as I screamed, "I am!" Finally, when there was no push left in us and our legs felt as weak as water, we'd break down crying and scoot around the bottom of the door. When Daddy settled down, and things would quiet, I'd crawl over into the corner of the room and bury my head in my legs until the police arrived or a neighbor appeared.

But this night as Mom gathered us round to pray for Daddy, I asked her, "How long will it be?"

"How long will what be, Honey?"

"You keep telling us to pray, every day, so Daddy will get saved and quit being mean. Well, how long is it till Daddy gets saved?"

I will never forget the answer my mother gave. I just accepted it then because she was Mom. I asked her a question; she answered. It had to be right – she was *Mom*. But I now understand, not only was she Mom, she was a praying mom. That was how she knew the words to say. She opened her mouth and let Jesus fill it with *His* answer.

"I don't know exactly which day it will be when Daddy asks Jesus into his heart. All I know is that Jesus *promised* it will come if we keep praying, so that is what we will continue doing. You just help me pray every night and let Jesus take care of Daddy, okay?"

That was fine with me. And pray we did! Our prayers continued over the next six years. As I look back over that period in my life I think, *Wow . . . my mom really had some awesome faith!* There are people who pray about things in

1

their lives and pray earnestly, for the first two weeks. But if God doesn't move within that fourteen-day period, that is it. How long does He expect you to wait anyway?

There are people who pray about things in their lives and pray earnestly, for the first two weeks. But if God doesn't move within that fourteen-day period, that is it.

But my mother never wavered, therefore, neither did I. She said Jesus promised He would save my daddy, so I knew if Jesus had promised it, there was no question. It would happen. Oh, I can hear the mind-wheels of the skeptic turning right now. Let me say to you: no, my mother did not lie. Jesus did promise this, in writing, and not to our household alone (Acts 16:31).

He promised you that too, if you choose to walk in His promise and stand faithful.

So, what happened with my dad? Well, as we prayed over the next year or so, he got worse. Isn't that how Satan usually works? Then we moved. I don't remember the circumstances of why we moved, but we moved, and Dad lost the job he had (where his drinking buddies were). When we moved, we just *happened* (if you believe in chance – I believe in divine appointment) to move to a neighborhood with a small community church on the street below our house. It was so close that at the age of seven, it was perfectly safe for me to ride my bicycle there. My mother was expecting another child, and she could not always take us. So, my brothers and I would hop aboard our bikes on those Sundays and Wednesdays and go on. Eventually, Dad got to where he'd go occasionally, whenever he was able to sober up enough from his Saturday night usual. He knew how badly we all wanted him to go, and the pastor made him feel welcome when he went. Pastor Barney knew Dad was far from being a saved man, but still he honored my dad, and Dad had a deep respect for our pastor.

A few more years passed. We were still attending that same little church, although we had once again moved. Then one evening, as my mother was cleaning the kitchen and my younger brother and I played cops and robbers with our five small kittens (don't ask – you do not want to know what we put those poor little creatures through, stuffing them into covered wagons and horse-drawn buggies), Dad was watching television and having his usual beer and peanuts cocktail. All at once, there was a great commotion and I heard Mom yelling with a rather panic-stricken voice, "Bill are you okay? Can you speak?"

As I turned, Dad was jumping up from the sofa with his hand over his chest beating it. His face was blood red and his eyes bulging out as though they were ready to pop right off his face. Every now and then he'd manage to draw a breath and say, "Judy, call the pastor." Each time he got the words out, Mom would answer, "Do I need to get an ambulance?"

Finally, as she ran into the kitchen and grabbed the phone book (there was no such number as 9-1-1 back then), Dad said, as he gasped for another breath, "If you don't call the pastor right now, I will be dead when the ambulance arrives."

By the time those words sprang forth from Dad's mouth, Mom had phone in hand and was dialing our pastor's home. As Pastor Barney answered, Mom began to explain what was happening. He had her quickly place the phone to Dad's ear. What happened next was nothing short of a miracle.

My little brother and I sat in the living room, observing all that was taking place and crying; not knowing if we'd see our daddy alive much longer. I listened as Dad reiterated to our pastor how he was popping peanuts and chasing them with beer. "Then," he said "I can't explain it, but all at once it felt like something grabbed my throat and began squeezing it shut. I wasn't choking on a peanut, but I knew I would if it didn't stop."

He continued talking, as the choking sensation would come and go, explaining to Pastor Barney all he could think about during this time was the fact that if he died he knew he'd "split hell wide open." He told our pastor he remembered walking down the church aisle as a little boy and asking the Lord to come into his heart, but then he

4

said, "Even though I walked the aisle, I'm telling you right now, if I die I know I will not make it to Heaven."

That night my brother, my mother, and myself all listened as our dear little pastor spent quite a while on the phone, leading my father through the sinner's prayer and explaining this brand-new way of life to him. I will never forget what happened after Dad hung up the phone. By the way, all symptoms of choking and death's grip ended as Pastor Barney led Dad through the prayer of salvation. My dad laid down the phone, turned to my mother and said, "Come on, Honey; I need your help."

My brother and I followed them into the kitchen and watched as Dad rounded up all the beer he had in the house and sat it at the sink. He and Mom stood there popping lid after lid and pouring each beer down the drain until our house was totally free of what my dad later referred to as "devil juice."

Watching from the sideline, my little brother said, "Are you going to be in trouble Daddy?" He knew if anyone wasted any of our father's beer, they would be in big, big trouble.

But that day my dad answered with, "No son. Your daddy won't be touching this stuff anymore. It's from the devil, and I don't want him anywhere near my home ever again."

David said, "Me neither!" then ran back to play. Me? Oh, I just kept watching Mom and Dad, all the while, at age eleven, thinking, *Wow Lord, You really are something.*

This is the day you told Mom about. The day we would see our daddy give his heart and life to You!

No one anywhere in all of creation could have loved their Heavenly Father or their earthly father more than I did that day. And my dad's salvation was real. After more than twenty-five years of drinking, Dad never touched alcohol again. He never attended rehab or an AA meeting. He just filled his life daily with God's Word and weekly with God's House. From that day forward, every time the sun would set, I'd leave whatever I was doing and run to the living room window and gaze out into the driveway. My little brother would see me and run into the living room, "Is it Daddy? Is it, huh?"

"Hush," I'd say. "I'll tell you when he pulls up." We knew every evening our daddy would be home straight after work, and we always greeted him at the front door. My little brother never knew what it was like to shake and shudder, wondering if Dad would even come home. For after that wonderful heavenly encounter in our living room that night, my "old" dad died, and I had a brand-new daddy. All to the glory of God!

Until God laid it on my heart to include this testimony in this book for the benefit of those having to live like we did, we never looked back at the "old way of life" or pondered upon the hurt and pain. For you see, when God makes all things new, He throws all the old junk, including the hurt, bitterness, anxiety, and hate as far as the east is from the west . . . never to be remembered again. Why on earth would you want to anyway? God's way, trust me, is *so* much greater.

For you see, when God makes all things new, He throws all the old junk, including the hurt, bitterness, anxiety, and hate as far as the east is from the west . . . never to be remembered again. Why on earth would you want to anyway?

I've met many people along life's way and heard thousands of testimonies of those rescued from life's treacherous gutters who were torn from Satan's very grip. As a young person, I used to wonder what it would be like to be some of those people and experience all the horrific things they had encountered such as drug abuse, sexual promiscuity, or alcoholism.

In my mid-twenties I would sometimes think, "I don't really even have a testimony to share with others. All I can say is I love the Lord and cannot recall a time in my life when He hasn't been there for me." Whee, some testimony; makes you want to shout, huh?

A few times, I even had thoughts go through my mind that maybe I should do something really, really stupid just one time and then turn it all back over to the Lord so I'd have a testimony to share.

My husband and I have worked with children of all ages over the years. Sometimes I would wonder, with the older kids, if we were even effective in helping them deal with a lot of the issues young people face today. Neither of us have ever taken drugs or ventured too far into sin. I did have a time in my life where I was confronted with the issue of alcohol and had to work through it and make a decision. It took about fifteen months, but as always, the Holy Spirit brought conviction, and the Lord lovingly reminded me I am His and He is mine. I had to learn that strongholds must be broken off your life, and the curse of the bloodline be destroyed through God's mercy and grace. Then, once again, I knew there was nothing in life that mattered more than my relationship with God.

And I had a very difficult time understanding "wishy-washy" Christians or those with addictions or hang-ups—those not 100% sold, and God forbid the poor little "struggling" Christians. If they would just totally commit everything in their life to Christ, they would be fine – all the time, through everything, no matter what. They were not really Christians; that's what it was. After all, I knew. I was 100% sold, without a doubt, born again, and probably God's best friend. And I knew there was really no such thing as a faltering Christian. You either loved the Lord and lived up to His name, or you were deceived and only thought you were on your way to Heaven but would one day be awakened to the resounding truth you are not the Christian you thought you were and probably not even saved.

How did I know?

I watched, as you attended only Sunday morning services and, on occasion, Sunday or Wednesday nights. I saw when you skipped church to go on a shopping trip or boat ride instead, and definitely on those occasions you chose worldly outings or a day of leisure at home rather than attending church functions. Yes, you were not acting "Christ-like" and could not possibly be sold on Him. Therefore, you were not a Christian. Thus saith Mandy!

⚸ Then … Came the Summer of 2002 ⚸

The year 2002 was one I will never forget. It was a time that forever changed my life, my outlook on life, my perspective of people, and my perception of "church people."

Someone asked me a while back how things were going with me now. We've been friends for many years. We worked together more than fifteen years in ministry at a national youth camp, and we were much more than mere camp acquaintances. That friend was an evangelist for many years, so it wasn't like we could get together often or visit frequently, yet the bond was so close I could feel the love and friendship 365 days a year, even if I only physically saw the friend once a year. Do you have a friend in your life like that? One so special that any time you have an opportunity to get together, it's like "ole times" and you simply pick up where you last left off, even if it's three years later?

Allow me to share a word of advice, coming straight from the heart of a gal who has tread some pretty deep "life" waters, so I say this with complete sincerity. If you are fortunate enough to have one of those friends, stop a moment, lift your hands toward Heaven and thank God for that friend. Most importantly, never, ever take that friendship for granted.

You may not have even given much thought to that friendship before reading this story because the bond is so sweet you never have to wonder if your friend will be there; he or she just always is. I didn't give enough thought to my friends either, until after the "crash" …

Have you ever met someone who was involved in a terrible accident? One so severe they were left with critical injuries, and it was uncertain if they'd ever walk again or regain the capacity to function normally? As you watched that person struggle to make the slightest accomplishment such as waving a hand or taking a cool sip of water, did you sigh a prayer, "Help them Lord," and feel your heart overcome with compassion? Were you praying for God to grant that person a miraculous recovery? If yes, God bless you. For you see, that person was me (spiritually) after the crash in the summer of 2002. Bear with me between these first two chapters as the story unfolds.

Everything seemed so perfect. Life couldn't be better. My husband and I had sold our home and temporarily moved into our rental property to fix it up and begin looking for a new house in the area we could call our retirement spot. We had moved around so much, it was really starting to get the best of all of us, and we made a promise to our boys that no matter what life dealt, we would remain in this community until they both finished high school. I know what it feels like to move around constantly and feel as though you'll never develop roots.

While I was growing up, my parents moved quite often. I didn't understand at the time that buying and selling property for profit was what allowed Mom to stay home with us kids. All I knew was I attended seven schools before I graduated from high school. I was a quiet kid and pretty much kept to myself. I made friends at every school, but never had any close friendships. That's a little difficult to do when you are never around very long. I remember starting eighth grade in a new school (again). That was the hardest transition I'd ever made. The previous school was one I had actually gotten to attend for four years, a record. I had finally started to feel secure in the fact that maybe, just maybe, this was it – the school I'd get to go to forever. I let my guard down and even had friends I'd call on the phone and have stay-overs with. Then, one fateful day . . .

"Mandy, come take a drive with us. We want to show you something."

"Okay, what is it?" I asked, wondering what the occasion was. Maybe we were going to get a new dog. Ours had gotten run over by the garbage man. Princess was her name. I loved her so much. I had no sisters growing up, only brothers, and my whole life I wanted a sister. As a kid, I used to go every Christmas to the shopping center and sit on Santa's knee. Every Christmas, I knew exactly what I wanted. I begged Mom and Dad for this one gift, just *one*. It was all I ever asked for but would never get. So, I had begun asking Santa for it too. Most kids, if their parents allow them to, believe in Santa and really put stake in what they ask him for. I on the other hand, never had a problem releasing the idea of his existence. He was just a mere man who added fun to the holidays but had no real power. Because every year I asked for the same simple gift from him, and every year got the same ridiculous answer.

"Ho, ho little girl. Come sit on Santa's lap. What is your name?"

"Mandy."

"Sandy?"

"No, Mandy. M-a-n-d-y."

"Oh, Mandy. That's an unusual name. Haven't heard that one much. Well, Mandy have you been a good girl this year?"

"Yes, Santa."

"Well, good little girls deserve nice gifts at Christmas. What would you like Santa to bring you this year?" and then, "Ho, ho, ho – I don't think Santa heard you right. What did you say you wanted?"

"A sister."

"Ho, ho, huuuh? Well now Sandy."

"Mandy."

"Yeah, whatever. I love giving good little girls nice gifts at Christmas, but there are some gifts that just can't come from Santa. Why don't we …"

"I know. Ask my mom and dad for this gift. It's one only they supposedly can give. I've heard that one before."

"Well, have you asked them?"

"Yes, and I *never* will ask again."

"Why not? What did they do when you asked them?"

"They gave me – HIM! The baby mom is holding in her arms, another brother!"

So, needless to say, that was the last year I had that conversation with either Santa or my parents. I felt I was probably much better off settling for the fact I would never have a sister to share my life with— to do girl things with

13

like trying out new hairstyles or applying make-up for the first time or going shopping together and discussing new boyfriends.

I was destined to a life of being "one of the guys," and that was exactly how I lived the early years of my life. I was afraid to let girl-friends in, for fear we'd become close, and I'd then move away. So, my childhood years were filled with baseball and football games, shooting hoops and boxing matches. I did fight the girls at least, and upon one occasion was left with a beautiful shiner to show off for weeks. To this day I can look at it on our old home movies and see the thin little gal with sun-darkened skin, scraggly hair, and the big black-n-blue shiner rounding her eye.

Don't feel too badly for me though. As I look back through my childhood days, I must say, over all, they were pretty good ones. I became our neighborhood babysitter at age thirteen and would watch sometimes as many as ten kids at once and enjoyed it. I guess my lady-like instincts still developed properly, even without my dream ever coming true of having a sister.

And, in getting back to the story, yes – the ride with Mom and Dad did end in yet another move and another school. But that is now long (very long) behind me. I survived. And as I grew and matured into an adult, I found that physically moving, losing friends, and trying to make new ones was easy compared to what you walk through later in life ... especially as a Christian who loves the Lord and wants to serve Him and have a relationship with others who feel the same.

For through it all, the Lord remains faithful, through every trial and in our times of struggle. We will see, if only we will hold on, persevere and endure, it will be… all for the glory of God!

STUDY GUIDE

❧ *Chapter 1* ❧

The Question Was Asked

(Answer these questions in your own way, then compare your answers with those given in Chapter 2. There are no right or wrong answers. However, we will search God's Word for His understanding in each area as we cover it. You will never go wrong if you stand on His Word.)

01) How would <u>you</u> define a Christian?

02) What do you look for in the life of a person to determine if Christ lives within him or her?

03) Have you known someone, a friend or perhaps even family member, who has been radically saved? Share how you <u>knew</u> Christ had become #1 in his or her heart.

04) Please take time to remember your salvation experience: (reminisce for a moment of that glorious day you asked Jesus to become Lord and Savior of your life).

How did you *know*, for a fact, He came to live within your heart?

05) Where are you today (at this very moment) in your walk with the Lord?

06) Do you desire more in your relationship with Him? List some of the "more" you hunger for:

God loves you and has a wonderful plan for your life. Stay close to Him.

Listen to His voice. Focus on what He is saying. How? Through His precious Word.

Absolutely every need you have, or will ever encounter, has been dealt with and overcome. As His Word becomes living revelation, you will see Him in His glory–as never before!

Let's continue . . .

Lord Jesus,

As I enter the next chapter of this book, help me to open my heart fully unto You and what You have to say. Speak into my life, Father, and give me spiritual understanding that I may know what is Your divine purpose and plan.

If I have had a problem in understanding Your Word, or if Your holy Word has never become "living" revelation in my life, I pray today will be the day, Lord. Open my understanding in a greater way than ever before.

Help me to see You in Your fullness. In Christ's precious name I pray. AMEN.

Chapter 2

QUESTION ANSWERED

T he question was asked. How would *you* define a Christian? I'm a Christian. I love the Lord and want to please Him, but for this period of more than six years, my life did not equal the standards I had always set for others to live up to. Those Christians whom I looked at and so quickly judged and determined their destiny. Instantly, without even knowing them, I, within myself, judged where they stood with God and whether they would make it to that eternal Heaven with the Lord– or were even worthy to bear His name.

When my friend asked this question, it was not one to be answered half-heartedly. She did not ask to be cocky or tear down someone's religious theology. She came to me completely grieved, at the lowest time of her life. She felt as though she had not only let God down but also everyone who had ever been a part of her life, including her family – her remaining family. For this question was asked shortly after she had lost her only son. He had just stepped out of his teen years and, within a short time, slipped into eternity.

All I could think was, *Jesus help me to be so careful not to offer merely my words or thoughts. Rather, please give me Your wisdom to offer Your words, for they bring life and healing.* I knew I could give her a slightly impressive "Mandy" interpretation of what being a Christian actually means, throwing in a few scriptures and making it sound sovereignly biblical – but upon offering her this, I would be giving unto my dear friend a bunch of empty words. I could mean well, but even with deepest sincerity they would remain lifeless words.

I've met a lot of well-meaning people who gave lifeless words to many. Although they were earnest in doing so, there was absolutely no fruit that came forth from the exchange. However, I've met others who have fallen on their face before God, refusing to give an answer to man until they clearly heard the voice of God. I've seen His words produce life and health; healing marriages and breaking addictions. I've watched in awe as those whom I never dreamed it was possible to see saved walked the aisle (in some cases running), laying down the "old man" and beginning as a new creation in Christ Jesus.

That, my friend, is the life of a true Christian.

Please know that giving your heart totally over to Christ does not mean you are now exempt from life's worries and cares. It does mean, however, you belong to a new family. You have a Father who is ever walking with you, praying and interceding on your behalf. He is a Father who will never leave you nor forsake you – that is His promise to you found in Hebrews 13:5. Though others may hurt and disappoint you, and brothers and sisters in Christ may turn against you, always know your loving, Heavenly Father is ever looking down with arms outstretched saying "I am still here. I'm rooting for you. Hang on – I'm sending help. Don't give up! You are mine, and if you will continue to trust Me right now, at your lowest point, I'll prove to you again and again how very much I love you."

I can testify – He will! Furthermore, He will not leave you at that place you are at right now. He will restore in such a way that when it's over and deliverance has come, you will realize there is a God in Heaven, and He loves you with total abandon!

⋇ ⋇

A few years ago, the Lord moved my family and me from a church we had been members of and served in for over six years. I know, I can hear the questions forming now: "What happened? Was there a church split, a 'nosey-roller,' a 'busy-brethren' – who did what to you there?" I hope it does not disappoint you when I say no one wronged us in any way. They did us *right*; up until the very moment we left.

Isn't that amazing? I know exactly why the first thought that comes to mind when someone decides to leave a fellowship of believers is "what brother or sister in Christ chewed you up and spit you out?" Because much too often, that is exactly what happens. God help us Christians that we may become more like *Him* and less like our flesh.

Let me share with you the events that led to our departure.

My husband and I have always been first in love with Christ, then in love with each other. We met at God's House, worked in ministry together, became best friends, shared with each other our likes and dislikes about all those we dated, and eventually knew and cared so much for each other there was nowhere else left to go!

After two and a half years of friendship, one and a half years of courtship, and a six-month engagement (hey, we had to make sure), we found ourselves saying the two most powerful words that have been spoken by mankind. "I do."

We continued working with kids of all ages. Whatever age group existed at the ministry God planted us in, we'd just go at it. See a need, fill a need. Each time God placed us in a church home, we'd say "This is it. This is where we'll serve until we retire!"

First, may I share with you a simple heavenly fact you learn after serving in ministry a while: there is no such thing as retirement in Heaven! Each time you "retire" from a branch of ministry you've served in (whether it be from hurt, being tired, or aging), God just prunes you, sticks your total being down into His Holy Ghost cup, and pours in the oil and the wine. Soon, out sprout new roots, reaching and searching for good soil to grow in. Then, God opens the door to the new phase of ministry He has for you. Retire? Ha, let's laugh in the face of the devil. He can retire any time he wants, but God's children are never retired. When we're worn out, stressed out, feeling aged or a little down, we get re-fired! That is the difference in the spirit-led life.

As we worked together in ministry, we found over the years that often, that which you think will *never* change in a church, can change overnight. Some changes are good, others ugly – and some, down-right devastating.

*that which you think will never change
in a church, can change overnight.
Some changes are good, others ugly
– and some, down-right devastating.*

When God led us to the church I have just referred to, He did so out of tremendous love. We had gone through a very bludgeoning hurt within a church family. It was one from which I thought I'd never recover, and probably would not have had it not been for God's amazing love and awesome power.

Little by little, I felt my zeal for God chipping away. My energy—spiritually, emotionally, and finally physically—drained from my entire being. Soon, I was much like the victim of a severe injury or a crippling illness, with uncertainty of what the future would hold.

Although this "crash" came seemingly all at once, knocking me off my feet, it did not happen from one blow. It was a chain of events which, link by link, wrapped themselves around my life until I was completely bound.

We had just moved and were feeling a little displaced. I had become very close to a woman for whom I had worked at a stock brokerage firm. She and her husband not only hired and trained me in the business, but they also took time to mentor me in Christ. It was such a way of life for them that I don't think they even realized the impact they were making. For me however, having just burst through my teen years and being at a place in God where I knew Him but didn't quite know how some Christians could be so "different" and so "in touch" with Him, these Christian business leaders made a lasting impression.

My employer would call me back to her office and ask if I'd like to have lunch with her and her husband. We'd talk a minute or two about our clientele and happenings of the day, then either she or her husband would say, "Oh, I have to tell you what God showed me." They'd begin talking about the Lord and His faithfulness, and I would listen, all the while thinking *Jesus, please give me that kind of relationship with You.*

I was sitting at the front desk one day humming to a Nancy Harmon song. Suddenly, I heard my boss calling for me from the back of the building. I knew she and her husband had been up to something for several days. There had been commotion and hammering going on above my head, but they had not uttered a word of their doings.

As I stood in the dark, almost bare storage room area of the old building, she said, "Look up." She and her husband began lifting their heads high. I followed in motion. Eyes lifting, focusing high – higher – then, "Whoa. What is that light?" I asked.

"It's our upper room."

"Our what?"

They began to explain how the Lord had laid it upon their hearts to make a room in the upper part of the back of the building where it would be totally quiet, peaceful, and away from all interruptions. The room was dimly lit, enough for reading, or you could leave all lights off and receive just enough of a peek of light from the city street that it was not completely blackened (a perfect prayer setting).

The décor was fashioned for comfort. As you entered the room, the most awesome feeling you could ever hope to encounter settled over you and within you. It was beyond description. As I walked into the room, tears filled my eyes. "This is Your room, isn't it Lord?" I felt Him so sweetly. I walked over, grabbed a couple of cushions, and sat on the floor of the upper room, looking out over the city streets and alley way.

"What did it feel like when You sat in the upper room, Lord?" I pondered upon what His thoughts might have been, while I basked in a glorious intimate moment with my Savior. It was unlike anything I had ever experienced. As I sat that evening peering out into the city, I felt such warmth, peace, and safety as though Jesus had wrapped His arms around me – spending time with *me* as I spent time with Him.

Many evenings were spent in that upper room while working at the brokerage firm. When the day came to say good-bye, I left with some most precious memories. I felt blessed to have been mentored by those who drew me ever closer to Christ. I had gained a true revelation of how real God's presence is and how much He desires our fellowship. I also wondered if I'd ever walk into a place again where God's presence would be so strong that His glory filled the room, as it did there, high above our office in that upper room.

Now, three and a half years later, much had changed. That employer had become a new mom and decided against returning to work. I left the brokerage firm, but my ex-boss's husband was now our pastor and had married Tom and me. They had started a church in the South Knoxville area where we faithfully attended, helping in every way we could. However, after more than three years of prayer, visitation, and advertising in the community, they did not feel they had gotten a positive enough response to continue. The ministry ended. We said our farewells and then decided upon a move to another county. We settled in, then began our search for a new church home.

I had heard of a church in the community that had ties to a sister church I had attended in a nearby town as a teen, so feeling it would be doctrinally sound, we began attending this new little fellowship. It didn't take long until we felt right at home. The pastor and his wife were close to our ages and were tremendously dedicated to the church. Everyone in leadership was strong in the Lord and loved one another with a real Christ-like love. We could not have been happier! We also became part of an excellent children's ministry, took a trip to Willie George Ministries in Oklahoma, and were on fire, glowing and blowing, seeking to do whatever God would have us do.

But something strange started happening. There was a sense that could be felt but not understood. We had now been active members at this church for over three years. We were expecting our second child and knew changes were taking place in our lives personally, but even more so in the ministry we were a part of.

As we entered church this particular Sunday, the pastor seemed distant, and his wife was out of view. Everyone knew something was up, but no one said a word. There was a sternness in the air as we waited to see what was taking place.

"Good morning."

"Good morning Pastor." Everyone echoed.

"I have some news. I know some of you have felt a sense of change lately, and now the time has come to confront you with the matter. I am stepping down as pastor of this congregation."

Shockwaves hit the atmosphere. You could feel them bursting through the thick tenseness that had enveloped the sanctuary. What would we do without a pastor? Would the church continue? They had begun this ministry, so would the doors close? And *who* would become our pastor? We loved them and could not fathom someone else in their stead.

The pastor continued speaking. He told of how he and his wife had poured their lives, hearts, and souls into this ministry for the past six years—how they had even given up their jobs and moved into the church to make ends meet so they could pastor full time and "prepare" the congregation for all God desired to do. And He did want to use that church. It was obvious. Many things had happened during the three and a half years we were there. It was evident God was moving. But now, something was wrong.

As the pastor spoke, he declared how hard he and his wife had worked trying to get everyone "at that level in God" where they so needed to be. He then stated he was at the point of being fed up with us and had told his wife he was ready to close the doors. He then ended his speech by saying, "But my wife, being the loving person she is, said we could not do that. She said, 'Go ahead and let go and turn the reigns over to me. I'll pastor them and continue this work you started.'"

We were then introduced to our "new" pastor, the pastor who would *put up with* us. Everyone applauded as she came forward and began to pour her heart out as to why God had led her to carry on this burden. She explained that many changes would begin to take place that would "improve" the ministry. She asked that we not buck at them, but rather embrace them, stating upon doing so we would begin to see a much better developed church.

However, as time went on, things got more and more out of hand. The Spirit of God that once moved so strongly in our midst diminished and a controlling spirit, with man-made rules, governed the body, replacing the leading of the Lord. We, along with others, suffered much hurt at the hands of this pastor due to dictates and demands that were extremely harsh and not conveyed with the love of Christ.

Upon leaving that ministry, we thought we surely would never have to worry about such brutality in God's House again. We were wiser and much more cautious spiritually. We were very careful, but we were also extremely skeptical.

As time passed, we visited several churches, finding a larger congregation where no one knew us, spoke to us or hardly even acknowledged our presence. Due to the tremendous hurt and spiritual battering we had endured at the hands of our former "new" pastor, we decided this church, where we were non-existent, was perfect. We could love the Lord, attend His House, and not have to worry about the way we were treated because we were seemingly invisible.

This plan worked fine for about eight months. See, God knows us even better than we know ourselves. He knew we needed time to heal from the wounds and get back on our feet. So, He allowed us to rest for a season, remain calm, be quiet, and let His gentle Holy Spirit feed us nuggets to sustain our spirits.

This year had also proven to be very trying at home as well. Almost from the time of birth, our second baby had health issues. At six weeks old, he suffered a seizure. Because of the uncertainty as to what caused this neurological event, we were given a prescription we had to keep with him at all times. If he started to run even the slightest temperature, it had to be administered immediately to avoid the possible recurrence of a seizure. The doctor told us if we kept him from any further seizures for the next (I think it was) 18 months, then the chances of the seizures ever returning were slim to none. The only problem was, he was always sick—always on the verge of fevers and always congested. To further complicate the matter, no one felt comfortable keeping him. The daycare he was in was one where I had placed him on its waiting list well before his birth to make sure he was with those who would properly care for him. But it got to the point they were calling once or twice weekly, asking me to come and pick him up because he was running a temperature. Finally, my doctor advised the best and possibly only real solution to getting him on solid ground was to remove him completely from the daycare setting. He was too susceptible to everything and needed to be kept in his own home environment for about a year.

The one problem the doctor did not understand was we could not survive on my husband's income alone. At eight months old, tubes were placed in Caleb's ears; this procedure made a big difference for a short period of time. Soon, I once again began receiving calls from the daycare center and realized I would have to find a job that would allow me to first be the mother God had called me to be and trust God to take care of the rest.

Thus, began my search for an evening job. I applied at all our local grocery and retail stores and, within days, received a part-time position at a small grocer near my home. The only negative I encountered in working there was the fact I had to be at work at 3:30 p.m. each day, and my husband didn't get home until about six o'clock. So, to take the job, I had to find someone who would watch my kids for a couple hours those three days per week, without charging full price. It seemed there was no one.

I was asking a close friend to help me pray about this dilemma, stating we really needed the extra income, and she said, "We have a lady in our church who recently opened a day care in her home, and she lives on the next road up from you. Let me tell her your plight and see if she may be able to help out." Within minutes, my phone rang.

"Grab a pen. She's going to take care of your babies and will only charge you hourly." What a blessing. Here just *happened* to be a lady who lived next to me that my friend knew from her church located another county away that was willing to do what no one in my town would do for me. Wow, God had once again moved on our behalf.

～❧ ❧～

As Felicia started watching my boys, she and I began talking and even started fellowshipping sometimes while the children played. She was one of those people you meet who has a dynamic outlook on life, an upbeat sense of humor, and a strong love for the Lord. We hit it off quickly and loved each other's company; and our kids loved playing together too.

I was amazed by her and her husband's love for their church. They talked about it all the time. Finally, I asked them what it was about their church that was so unique they would drive to another county, passing up umpteen churches to get there. They immediately began sharing of the closeness and love among the people and the sweet presence of God that resided there. That was it. I'd heard enough! I knew my husband and I had to check this place out for ourselves – and we did.

How refreshing it was. This small church was filled with a group of believers who, although they were lacking in number, had a huge handle on how to love the Lord and each other. After attending a short while, we began to feel at home. It was so wonderful to once again feel loved and acknowledged. It was awesome to again sense God's presence, wooing us back to that level in Him we once knew. Yes, this was what our spirit yearned for; this was what our hearts desired.

After attending the church for about a year, God laid it upon our hearts to begin a children's ministry. We were told the pastor and his wife would never go for it. This was something that had not been done there with any success and would more than likely not be permitted a second try. We were a little nervous about talking to them, having been told we may be turned down, nevertheless, God kept dealing with our hearts. We prepared an outline of how the ministry would reach the little ones with a message on their level, allowing them to understand a Savior who loves them and has a wonderful plan for their lives.

Finally, the day came. We presented the outline, and immediately our pastor said, "Fantastic. When do we start?" Thus, began our children's ministry. It started with five children of varied ages and proved to be quite challenging, but God was faithful. Within that first year, we watched the ministry grow from five to thirty-five, with two separate classes formed to better accommodate their ages. We were so excited, so in love with these kids and with all God was doing. Surely, we had found the place we would serve until the day we "retired" or expired—whichever came first!

The next five years were totally indescribable. God took our availability and desire in working with children and

escalated it to a level that only He could. We were con-
tacted by the national youth director from our church's
headquarters and asked to step in and help with the children's class at its annual youth camp. It was quite an experience. We ministered to approximately ninety children
between the ages of eight and twelve each day in a two-
hour class setting. We had no idea how to teach a group
this size, but once again, God so faithfully gave us His
capability. We worked together with the director, listened
as he shared the vision God had given him for this camp,
and brainstormed together, making sure we were flowing
within his God-given vision.

This prayerful collaboration is extremely important in any
ministry God calls you to. If you are not the director, you
must pray, converse with, and catch the vision of that leader
so you may go forth in unity. If you do not, everyone will
be pulling in a different direction, and even if all involved
mean well, soon the fabric of that ministry will fray.

We all worked together, year after year, praying and
seeking God to help us in reaching young people with the
life-changing message of God's love. After six years of
growth in ministry in our local church and within the national
level, once again change came knocking at our door.

The founder of our church's organization passed away, and
the reigns of leadership were turned over to new authority.
Although the founder had talked with all involved on the
leadership board, still in his passing, there was turmoil and
dissention between members as to how the ministry would

continue operating. Jealousy and mistrust sprang up, and soon, we found our church right in the middle of the chaos. We were approached by our pastor's wife. "We know how much you love your involvement with the national youth camp, but we can no longer support this organization. We are severing ties and ask that you carefully and prayerfully consider the same."

Surely not. Would we have to decide whether to leave our home church or walk away from this move God had placed us in for over six years? Not because God was calling us away, but because men could no longer get along with one another? God help us all. How unfair church disputes and divisions are – especially when the young, innocent lives of children are involved.

We did pray. We prayed very hard because we didn't want to lose our church family, but we also could not walk away from our dear brothers and sisters in Christ we were working with on the national level when God had not told us to walk away. We were working together, hand-in-hand and heart-to-heart, to make an eternal difference in the lives of young people.

We talked with our pastor and his wife and explained our position. We could not just walk away from the national youth ministry because of a church dispute when God had not released us. We asked for their understanding. They told us they would permit us to continue in it if we felt we must *but* made it very clear they would no longer support us in any way in this endeavor. This was tough, especially since they were the ones who had introduced us to it all in the first place, telling us what a mighty move of God it was. Now – we were suddenly alone. But that was okay, as long as they understood.

It wasn't long after this conversation that tension began building. We were finding ourselves on the defense, having to prove our integrity in situation after situation. Soon, we started to feel a tug at our hearts and knew God was preparing us for a possible move. Yet it was so difficult to believe God would want to move us away from a ministry He had led us to (now almost nine years ago) which had brought such healing and allowed us to reach so many young lives with His love.

Looking back, I realize had we listened intently to God's nudging and laid aside all feelings and emotions involved, things would have ended much differently. God would have already removed us before the mess hit. Yes, obedience *is* much better than sacrifice.

But we held on and continued trying to minister. Soon we were being met with offense on every side, and things grew very tense. We met with our pastor and his wife, but it was to no avail.

Another family in the church began rising against us and the offense was so deep, yet still we tried standing steadfast and pushing through opposition. We spent week after week defending our character and ministry . . . and then, the final blow fell.

Upon entering the parking lot this Sunday morning, we were met by our pastor and his wife. Accusations, criticisms, and every kind of ugly exchange the enemy could throw it seemed was dealt that day – before we could even enter God's House.

We were told if we chose to stay, we would need to sit in the back of the church until they decided how they would handle everything. So, there we stood, on the front steps of the church we had attended and ministered in, next to the pastor and his wife whom we had worked with side by side and proven ourselves to countlessly over the last nine years. We had served as both children's pastors and associate pastors for most of the time spent there. Now, we stood speechless and totally rejected by them.

We left that day with hearts torn and emotions shattered. I did not realize the toll I would allow it to take in my life. Little did I know how I would relive the facial expressions and harsh words of those we had so dearly loved, fingers pointing and accusations flying, replaying in my mind repeatedly, week after week – month after month – year after year.

Upon leaving that day I said, "Lord, this is it. I love You and will never walk away from You, but I *hate* church people. Please God, don't ask me to go back to church anywhere again. I can't take the pain involved in trying to serve You with other "so-called" Christians. And I cannot watch my boys *ever* have to go through anything like this – ever again!"

~~≈ ≈~~

After that summer of 2002, or the "Crash" as I refer to it, things in my walk with the Lord were not the same. Unknowingly, I allowed the tremendous hurt experienced there and previously, to overtake everything God had placed within me. I began pulling back from God little by little, until I had grown farther away than I ever dreamed possible. I had suffered such hurt at the hands of the female pastor, along with the devastating blow dealt to my family by those we dearly loved in ministry that I walked through time wandering aimlessly. Suddenly, I awoke one day and looked into the mirror of my life.

"My Lord – what has happened to me? Where am I (spiritually)? And who am I? What happened to that gal who once walked hand in hand with Jesus, loved people and ministry, and would *never* back down in the face of adversity?"

All I saw was this shell of a lady, a shell so hard there was no way to penetrate it with human hands. An occasional smile here or handshake there and then, back into the shell to retreat from all those who seemingly cared. At first, I tried acting as though things were fine. I would flash a smile whenever I had to. Someone would say, "How are you today?"

I would respond, "Great, thank you." All the while thinking, "Go away. Please, place that hand back in your pocket and save it for someone else. It hurts to be touched." All I wanted was to be somewhere where no one knew my name or cared, a place where we could keep our boys in church, because *they* needed it. Not me however, I was fine.

This, my friend, was the way I lived for over six years. As I pulled away from everything and everyone, I entered a path which led into a valley so deep and dark, I could have never fathomed going there and after a while, did not think I would ever escape.

After leaving the ministry we had served in for over nine years, we spent a solid year visiting church to church, and oh my, what an experience! It is amazing how different churches are. We went to a variety of denominations, non-denominations, and a few "in-betweens." Some we felt very welcomed in, others not so much. But we could not find one where we felt God's thumbprint of approval for our family. Our boys were at those very impressionable ages when all this happened, and to this day what I hate most about what the devil did is that it affected my sons so greatly. I love my boys and felt a lot like past vice-presidential nominee, Sarah Palin, when she expressed during a campaign speech, "The only difference between a hockey mom and a pit bull is lipstick." Well, I must say, that statement also stands for any mom whose kids have been attacked . . . and Christian moms are no exception!

In every church attended, we looked for a strong youth ministry for our oldest son and an effective children's church for our youngest. I even prayed with fervency, asking God to bless us with a church where our boys could be fed; and if we didn't get anything out of it, we'd be okay. Just take care of our boys, Lord.

But even at our lowest times, and through desperate prayers, we serve a loving God who whispers, "I have more for you."

But even at our lowest times, and through desperate prayers, we serve a loving God who whispers, "I have more for you." And at our family's point of spiritual desperation, He stepped in, leading us to a church with a strong youth ministry and an awesome children's church. In time, my husband even ended up pastoring the children. Me? Oh no, I had "retired" from ministry. The church loved our family and welcomed us into fellowship. They also tried for six years to reach into my life, but I had allowed the shell to harden that one area Christ warns us to protect – my heart. I had replayed the criticism, harsh words, and rejection for so long, they had crept down from my mind and settled into every chamber of my heart. I did not even realize the vast damage taking place.

Soon, my family was attending many services without me. I was beginning to suffer physical pain from a severe shoulder condition and was taking a host of medications. Prescription anti-inflammatory pills, along with prescription pain medication when severe; Aleve™ for constant lower back pain, Excedrin™ for headaches, sleeping pills to rest at night, and caffeine tablets to make it to work the next morning. I never felt rested, never felt well, and always had a justifiable excuse for missing church. When you are taking that much medication daily and working full time, there is always some reason you don't feel like sitting through a service. Looking back, I can tell you, as I speak now totally healed and freed of all medications, what I truly was suffering from (apart from the shoulder condition) were major depression and spiritual oppression. That, along with the other aches and pains were all merely symptoms of my troubled roots.

One day while driving home from work, tears filled my eyes – *my eyes*. You don't realize what a miracle that within itself was. I am not an emotional person by nature, but at that point in my life I had not shed a tear in years. I was so numb I couldn't feel emotional pain if I tried. Yet at that moment in my car as I drove down a little country back-road, tears began flowing, and I knew it was serious.

I cried out in desperation, asking God to please let me die. I saw no possible way I could ever be of use to His Kingdom again, and I did not want to bring Him shame. Then, in my despair I uttered one last plea, "Either let me die, or let me feel Your presence again Lord, because I cannot live this way." It had been so long. I'd had a few minor breakthroughs and felt His holy presence chip away some icy areas around my heart and mind, but still I was frigid inside. This had gone on so long that I honestly, before God, was afraid I was destined to never feel His love, power, or presence again – and let me tell you friend, that is a very scary place. Pray to God you never enter that valley. If you are there now, hang on, you are not reading this book by accident!

⚜

It was just a casual conversation that happened to take place (ordained by God is more like it). I was at a neighbor's house. As we chatted, her friend began talking about the new church in the area she was attending. She looked at me and said, "If you get a chance sometime, we'd love for you to visit with us." That was it. A simple open-ended invitation. Nothing would ever come from that would it? But what she didn't know was, God had been stirring things inside of me, even greater than I realized.

I had begun praying for direction. The boys were older now, not attending youth services, and the church we'd been a part of was in the next county over from where we lived. My husband had just stepped down from being children's pastor for five years, after feeling the Lord leading him to do so. He had talked with our pastor a year prior, but neither felt it was God's timing at that moment. Due to past experience in not handling things correctly a time or two, my husband knew you *do not* walk away from a ministry until God has sent a replacement. How will you know when it is God's perfect timing? When you can leave that ministry in capable hands to where no one is hurt in the process, especially when children are involved.

How will you know when it is God's perfect timing? When you can leave that ministry in capable hands to where no one is hurt in the process, especially when children are involved.

God did finally release him. The church made the formal announcement on a Sunday morning, my family and I attended the following two services, and then God led us to a church we'd call home. I know. You are thinking "That quick? Are you sure it was God?" Listen, our Heavenly Father knows us much better than we know ourselves. He knew I was struggling tremendously within my soul and desperately crying out for help, and He poured in the oil and the wine.

Isn't it funny how God moves? As His Word declares, His ways are high above ours. His wisdom never ceases to amaze me. Here I was, at the lowest point I'd ever been in my life. My husband had spent the year of 2008 in and out of work struggling to keep a job. We had planned to one day move closer to my parents to help them out in their later years, but at the moment did not want to move from the home we had begun calling our retirement spot. However, when 2008 rolled around we, along with much of the American population it seemed, were forced to move from our home into a less expensive one to make ends meet.

Our lives seemed to be crumbling around us and without realizing the extremity of it, I was slipping into a spiritual, mental, and emotional breakdown. As I cried out to God for help, I kept going down in life's sea of fear. I would bob back up and cry out and then go back down again, each time wondering if I'd have another spiritual breath left to cry out. But God is always faithful, and He had a plan.

After the hurt I had encountered by the pastor's wife and the devastating blow sustained at the hands of the female pastor previously, I vowed never to allow myself to get close to a pastor's wife again or a female pastor if I ever met another one. I held true to that vow for several years.

Now, as we prepared for bed on a Saturday night, my husband said, "Well, both boys are with friends tonight. It'll just be me and you at church tomorrow babe."

Suddenly I commented, "Why don't we go visit Paula's church? She invited us."

"That's fine with me, but are you *sure* you're okay with it?"

I then came to myself. What on earth was I saying? Go visit Paula's church? The one she had nonchalantly invited us to, probably just being nice? The one she told us all about and how God was moving and changing hearts and lives there? The one— she then told us – which had a *woman pastor*?

What on earth was I thinking? Why did I feel the urge to go there? Quick, there was still time to say, "Ha, just kidding. Had you going, huh?" But I couldn't.

"Yes, I want to visit."

And away we went to a brand-new house of fellowship. One which we knew absolutely nothing about. May I share with you, often, in those times when God leads you to a place you know nothing of, it is so His Holy Spirit can bring you to a place that only He knows of, and it is good! Little did I know the one area I had once been so tremendously hurt in would now be the area in which I would receive the most healing. What would it take to penetrate this hard, tough shell I had placed around my life physically, mentally, emotionally, and spiritually? God and the hand of His servant: a woman pastor!

~✺✺~

One last thought I must invoke here. Many days after writing this chapter, I was speaking with our former pastor from the church we had left. I was sharing with him how I knew our departure and going to the new church was a God-thing. I also briefly shared my testimony, the previous hurt encountered, and why I, within myself, would have never chosen this church. Suddenly, in the middle of my story, his voice burst across the phone lines. "Praise God, Sissy; it all makes sense now!"

"What, Pastor?"

"The reason you could not receive your total healing under this ministry." He asked if he could share something with me that a pastor friend of his had told him years ago. He continued, "I haven't thought of this story in years, until right now. This is awesome. You see, God knows all things and handles everything with great wisdom and care. The home of this pastor friend of mine was a half-way house, if you will, for foster children. His house was where they took children who were being abused in their homes and had to be removed. Upon removing them from the abusive situation, they were placed in my friend's home for nurturing and care, to prepare them for their new home. Upon first arriving, the children were scared and shaken. My friend told me each time they would take a new child in, knowing the severe pain and hurt they had been through, they would take them into that part of the home where they had been previously hurt. They would then care for them, in that very place, in the appropriate way, loving them and showing them they were now safe. They would keep the child in that place, continuously loving them, until that child was completely over his or her fear and began to feel comfortable. Then, they could release those children into that which would become their 'new home' – where they could grow and thrive and love again." My former pastor then added, "Our loving Heavenly Father cares for us in that same way. For that place where you have been most hurt is always the place God will send you back to receive your healing. So, you see, that is why God had to move you to where you are now to complete your healing. Your deepest hurt was at the hands of a woman pastor, and now your healing and deliverance will be completed through the loving care of a woman pastor."

For that place where you have been most hurt is always the place God will send you back to receive your healing.

In conclusion may I add, whatever place in your life where pain was inflicted, I pray God's almighty hand lead you to that "half-way house" where you can go and just be loved and cared for. Then, as you feel strengthened and a yearning begins for another level, my prayer is that God direct you to that special place you will call home. May it be there, you receive your complete healing in Him.

Isn't God good? He loves you with an unfathomable love. He alone knows how to lift you from that place in which you thought you'd never recover, and He will …

For your healing . . . and all for the glory of God!

That, dear friend, is the key: true repentance before God.

True repentance is to turn away from something *completely*. Repentance is not merely being sorry for what you've done or being sorry for being caught. Neither is it the fact you are sorry you partook of that thing; that is conviction – the seed planted within you, necessary for repentance, but repentance goes much deeper than saying "I'm sorry." Being sorry is not enough.

When we truly allow Christ to become Lord of our life, we encounter Him face-to-face. We *confess* our sins. We *repent* of all sins committed, and we *accept* Him as Lord. Laying *all* sin down, we walk away and begin our new, resurrected life in Christ. The old man is dead: dead to walking in those old paths and partaking of old habits, even dead to old desires. The new man seeks after things above. Colossians 3:1-3 reads "If then you were raised with Christ, seek those things which are above, where Christ is, sitting at the right hand of God. Set your mind on things above, not on things on the earth. For you died, and your life is hidden with Christ in God." And that is only the beginning. There is so much more God has in store for the life of a Christian.

02) In the first chapter, you were asked what you look for in the life of a person to determine if Christ lives in him. God's Word tells us we will know those who truly belong to Him. Let's look at the traits which distinguish a born-again believer:

LOVE: John 13:35–"By this all will know that you are My disciples, if you have love for one another."

FRUIT OF THE SPIRIT: Galatians 5:22-23–"But the fruit of the Spirit is love, joy, peace, longsuffering, kindness, goodness, faithfulness, gentleness, self-control. Against such there is no law."

A CRUCIFIED LIFE: Galatians 5:24–"And those who are Christ's have crucified the flesh with its passions and desires."

Lord Jesus,

Thank you for salvation! Thank you for this new life I now walk in. Please help me to understand all You have in store for me as Your child.

I repent of the old ways and habits I have held onto. Today, I lay them at Your feet. In Your strength, I will walk away and overcome. For Your Word declares, "I can do all things through Christ who strengthens me." (Phil. 4:13) I choose to live my life pleasing my Heavenly Father. When others look at my life, may they know I am Your disciple by my love. In Jesus's name I pray. Amen.

SO, WHO AM I?

There is a vast misconception many believers have fallen prey to by thinking if you give your heart to Jesus, turn everything over, and declare Him Lord and Savior, everything is roses from that moment on. The Bible does say if we confess our sins, He is faithful and just to forgive us our sins and cleanse us from all unrighteousness (1 John 1:9). So, in this respect things *are* great now. However, becoming a born-again believer does *not* exempt you from the trials of life. Never did scripture tell us this in any form or fashion. As a matter of fact, as you read the gospels and walk through Jesus's time of ministry here on earth, you will find He warned (and His disciples warned after His departure), that there *would be* trials and temptations, times of great sorrow, and obstacles to overcome. But, never did our Heavenly Father tell us this without giving us hope through Him:

> Matthew 5:11-12: "Blessed are you when they revile and persecute you, and say all kinds of evil against you falsely for My sake. Rejoice and be exceedingly glad, for great is your reward in Heaven, for so they persecuted the prophets who were before you."

John 16:33: "These things I have spoken to you, that in Me you may have peace. In the world you will have tribulation; but be of good cheer, I have overcome the world."

1 Peter 4:12: "Beloved, do not think it strange concerning the fiery trial which is to try you, as though some strange thing happened to you."

1 Peter 1:6-9: "[6]In this you greatly rejoice, though now for a little while, if need be, you have been grieved by various trials, [7]that the genuineness of your faith, being much more precious than gold that perishes, though it is tested by fire, may be found to praise, honor, and glory at the revelation of Jesus Christ, [8]whom having not seen you love. Though now you do not see Him, yet believing, you rejoice with joy inexpressible and full of glory, [9]receiving the end of your faith – the salvation of your souls."

That is what this walk with our loving Heavenly Father is all about! Yes, there will be times of testing and trials, but the word of God is a promise you can take to the bank. Listen to what the above scriptures in 1 Peter are saying. Let's closely examine them:

Verse 6: When trials or temptations come, remember this important fact: when it is God who is testing, it is always for the purpose of proving someone and *never* to cause him to fall. The devil brings temptation to try to cause one to fall, but God only and always does this to prove (or make sure of) your salvation!

Verse 7: When this test proving your faith comes, you look more precious to your Heavenly Father than gold which is tried in the fire (fire perfects and pulls out all the dross and makes the gold 100% pure). As you are being tried, Jesus looks down, expecting something glorious to be brought forth as all sin and imperfections are burned away. Your life and faith are now an offering worthy to be received and will bring glory and honor unto Christ.

Verse 8: You are now so close to your Heavenly Father that you love Him with your total being (though you have never beheld Him with human eyes, you *know* Him). For you've held tight to His hand and laid your head against His chest during this time. You believe, have a mental persuasion, and complete trust in Him, for you've felt His heart beat. Though others will not understand how you can love Him and trust Him during what they've seen you go through, they begin to observe that you are filled with a joy that you cannot express, that is full of glory. This is gladness of heart (not an emotional thing – a heart thing). You can do nothing but glorify your God, for now more than ever, you recognize who He is, and you freely give Him the full honor, love, and respect He is so deserving of.

Verse 9: And what does Christ give unto you in return? He gives the *end* of your faith. Oh, this doesn't mean an expiring of. It doesn't mean it's over or is something you will one day receive in glory. No, that will be in addition to what you experience here on earth. The word *end* here is derived from a word meaning "to reach the end goal or limit at which a person ceases to be what he was up to that point; at which point previous activities cease" (Zodhiates 1991, 1762). My friend, this trial was not to finish you off – it was to purify your life and make you into that child of God He fully intended you to be. You have reached that level in faith called total dependence on God. You now *know* you can fully rely on and trust in Him. You no longer have a little faith – you are a person of faith. You have reached that point where you have ceased being who you were, a Christian with a little faith in God. You have now received the completion of your faith and total deliverance for your soul. Please note, the word *salvation* here does not mean the day you accepted Christ. This usage of the word *salvation* actually means "total deliverance, salvation, and preservation of your body, mind, will, and emotions" (Zodhiates 1991, 1760). Through the testing of your faith, as you lean on your beloved Christ Jesus and lay your total self at His feet, He raises you up as a new person of faith. One who *knows* God is in complete control. As you glorify Him with the honor and love due His name, He burns everything out of you that is not Him. He completes your faith, seals your salvation, brings total deliverance, and preserves you – body, mind, will, and emotions. It is in Him you now live and move and have your being.

When trials come, you will no longer wonder, *am I really saved Lord?* When it seems that all of Heaven has dried up and all hell has broken loose, you will remember–this is the testing of my faith. It is not the end; it is rather my time to shine!

When it seems that all of Heaven has dried up and all hell has broken loose, you will remember–this is the testing of my faith. It is not the end; it is rather my time to shine!

So, what if the devil comes and tries to tell you, "You know you never really 'got it.' That's the whole problem here, you were never really saved." What do you do then?

Stop, drop, and roll! Everyone has been taught from an early age that is how you put out an unwelcome fire. Don't let it get out of hand. Don't allow the devil to pour his hellish fuel upon you and choke out that new life in Christ:

> **STOP** at the place you hear that voice speaking. Ask, "Spirit that is speaking to me now, do you profess that Jesus Christ came in the flesh to save all humanity?" No demonic spirit will hang around when faced with the precious name of Jesus.

> **DROP** to your knees and be still before God. Listen for His voice. Jesus said in John 10:14, 27, "I am the good shepherd; and I know my sheep, and am known by my own . . . My sheep hear my voice, and I know them, and they follow me." Ask God for greater discernment than ever before, so you may always know His voice and listen to no other.

> **ROLL** your life into the Word of God, reminding the devil you were bought and paid for as declared in John 3:16, "For God so loved the world that He gave his only begotten Son, that whoever believes in Him should not perish but have everlasting life."

Know your God. Put total faith and complete trust in Him and purpose in your heart that you will live for Him only, and no other will you serve. The Bible states in Philippians 2:12 we must work out our own salvation with fear and trembling. God knows those who have fully committed, asking Him to live in their heart and life, and meant it! He knows the voices or hearts of His sheep, and He does not look at the outward flesh, as we do, to decide who measures up. He looks at the heart.

Do you realize the one man in the Bible who God declared *"a man after His own heart"* was King David (1 Sam. 13:14)? Yes, the same David who lusted after Uriah's wife and sent Uriah off to battle to be killed so he could have her. Yes, the same David who ran from King Saul and feared for his own life at times. But you see, this was also the same David we see in Psalm who was quick to repent before His God because he knew from where his help came. And, this was the same David to whom God gave strength to kill a lion and a bear with his bare hands.

David was far, far from perfect in man's eyes, but his heart was pure. You can read many passages in Psalm and see there were times in David's life when he too questioned where he stood with God. Oh, what a cry of longing to know if everything was okay between him and His Heavenly Father. Let me tell you, crying out and asking God questions is okay. Don't ever let anyone tell you if you question God you are not saved. Nowhere in scripture do I find that questioning God reveals a lack of salvation. Never did He disown David when throughout the Book of

So, Who Am I?

Psalm David repeatedly cried out with loud Why's! Never did God respond with "How dare you question who I really am. Can't you see?"

No! When God looked down upon that heart that was totally honest and open, laying before His feet asking, "Why Lord?," the God of the universe – David's loving Heavenly Father – smiled and said, "There is a man after my own heart" (1 Sam. 13:14.)

Want to know how God feels about you right now? What His heart and thoughts are toward you? I know – He told me. He prophesied His thoughts to me about you. He said, "For I know the thoughts that I think toward you, says the Lord, thoughts of peace and not of evil, to give you a future and a hope" (Jer. 29:11).

See, He prophesied it to you, too, through His precious Word. It does not matter who you are, what you've done, or how messy your life may look right now. God loves you and has a beautiful plan for your life. He asks only one thing of you – give Him your all!

Some reading this may say, "Yeah, but I have absolutely nothing to offer Christ. I am a *nobody* with *no* talents and *no* means of obtaining any." Congratulations! You, my friend, are the most perfect candidate of all. When you surrender your all to Christ, He takes you, remakes you, and molds you into His perfect image. He doesn't need your capability – the Holy Ghost is your talent and grace, your ability. God needs your availability; nothing more and nothing less. As you lay down your flesh and allow the Holy Spirit to work and speak through you, you will begin to see God's perfect will accomplished here on earth as it is in Heaven.

He doesn't need your capability – the Holy Ghost is your talent and grace, your ability. God needs your availability; nothing more and nothing less.

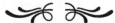

Knowing now who you are in Christ, no devil in hell (or your carnal, fleshly mind) can deter you from that great promise of salvation. Make sure your salvation. Walk in it 24/7. How? By establishing a personal relationship with Jesus Christ.

It doesn't matter how long you've been a Christian, we must all (myself included after more than forty-five years of salvation) make it a daily decision. *Today*, I am going to live for God and do all I can to further His Kingdom.

To all believers who have been held captive by Satan because of hurt you have gone through, I pray the words in this book minister and bring freedom, helping you to see how very loved by God you are. *You are special*, and whatever you've been through, please know God is greater.

Know you are not alone. And now, as you allow Him, your Heavenly Father wants to wrap His arms around you and hold you, reminding you His love is ever present, never ending, forever merciful, and totally unconditional.

Whatever life has thrown at you, whether it be hurt in church, rejection from family, or the devastating loss of a loved one, God has not left you. He understands, and when no one else can help, *He can*.

Today is a new day. Choose from this day forward to totally surrender your life as a living sacrifice – daily. Let your first "good morning" be to your Heavenly Father. Start each day by reading His Word. If not possible to do so in the mornings, make it a daily decision to find special time whether it be during afternoon lunch or at night when the kids are tucked in bed. Find that time to "enter into your closet" (Matt. 6:6 KJV) and meet one-on-one with your First Love.

Have you ever wondered why the Bible says to enter into your closet, or room, when you pray? Here is a thought to ponder that may forever change the way you pray!

Matthew 6:6 tells us, "But you, when you pray, go into your room, and when you have shut your door, pray to your Father who is in the secret place; and your Father who sees in secret will reward you openly."

If you study the word *room* here, going back to the original translation, I believe you will find it can also be translated as "storage room." And that "secret" place God resides in will, I believe, be found to also mean "storehouse." Therefore, it appears what Christ is showing us is that when we pray, entering into our "storage room" and shutting the world out, He meets us there. And in that special place where Heaven meets earth, He will take from *His* storehouse and place into our storage room all "things" that He has for us.

Envision, if you can, Christ taking all things that pertain to life and godliness from His secret place, or storehouse, and placing them within *you*, His chosen vessel who has taken time to meet with and receive from their Heavenly Father – Wow! That is true intercession. That is a love that absolutely no one can match. What a Savior! What a mighty God we serve!

And once you are walking with Him daily, visiting Him in your prayer closet, and drawing so close to His loving presence, there is one last thing of great importance you must do as a child of God. That is "not forsaking the assembling of ourselves together, as is the manner of some, but exhorting one another, and so much the more as you see the Day approaching" (Heb. 10:25).

I know, I felt that cold chill. Many of you have gone through much hurt in the Church, and the last thing you want to do is go back to God's House for more. Believe me, I know how you feel, and I know for you to do this, God will have to intervene.

There is a corporate anointing that can only be received by blending hearts and spirits together as one unto God.

I can tell you, in full confidence of my Savior, *He will.* When He asked you to enter your prayer closet, it was for your good, so His blessings may overtake you and consume you. That is also the reason He asks you to assemble in His House with other believers. There is a corporate anointing that can only be received by blending hearts and spirits together as one unto God. I am not saying you are not saved if you decide to serve God from home. I *am* saying however, from what I see expressed in His Word and from personal experience, you are missing out on so many awesome blessings and unique gifts God has for your life by allowing the devil and/or flesh to keep you away from other believers and out of God's House.

Let me be very clear at this point. When you pray and allow God to lead you to that house of fellowship where He truly wants you to be, you will know it by the fruit you see in that ministry. When you enter a house of worship where God can be God, the Holy Spirit is welcome, and the people hunger to be like Him – you will feel Christ's awesome, glorious presence, and you will *know* God abides there and you are "home."

Ever wonder if you are in the right church? Here is a good way to determine just that. You will know you are in the right church when you can't wait to get there and can't stand to leave! That's how it feels when you are truly in your Father's house.

And now, before God, I must give a crucial warning to all pastors and leaders in churches throughout America. While writing this book, God laid so strongly upon my heart the condition that many of His churches are in today. He began reminding me of ministries I have been a part of or have heard of through other pastors, organizations, friends, and acquaintances. My heart broke as I saw the way He sees His house and His people today.

I've had much experience helping with new ministries. I have seen all they go through trying to meet the challenge of establishing the vision God has given. I've watched large ministries as they endeavor to keep everything under control and hold onto their vision purposed by God. I have seen some who have spectacularly met and exceeded all expectations, keeping their heart right on track with the very heartbeat of God; and I've seen others who have failed miserably, massacring and destroying the spirits of many God had called to work alongside them. Losing not only the vision God placed within them, but their victory as well. The very foundation of the ministry crumbling, I've watched as many hurt and wounded sheep scattered abroad, hoping, and praying God would intervene in their lives lest they never recover from such devastation.

God never intended for His House to be a house of hurt. He does not take pleasure in an establishment that calls itself a church but offers no help to the hurting or out-stretched arms to those in need. God declared His House shall be "…a house of prayer for all nations" (Mark 11:17). When He came across those using it for reasons other than that, He destroyed those things that stood in place of His glory (Mark 11:15-17).

God never intended for His House to be a house of hurt. He does not take pleasure in an establishment that calls itself a church but offers no help to the hurting or outstretched arms to those in need.

We all need God. We all need His House, and we all need each other. However, before we can adequately fulfill the vision or mandate God has placed within us, we must be certain we are doing all things as unto Him, and all for His glory.

As we read in Revelation, we see the seven churches and their attributes, both good and bad, and we also see what

God's thoughts toward them were. As God spoke to my heart about His Church today, I began seeing them through His eyes; much as He saw the churches in Revelation.

First, there is the church of the **"Give Up Spirit"**:

This church is a ministry that came to town with tremendous fire and zeal. God placed a vision within that leader, directed him to the appropriate location, and began moving by His Spirit and power as worshipers gathered.

However, as time passed week after week, month after month, and now year after year, their flame of fire is but a flicker, and their zeal has turned to defeat. They are not seeing the numbers come as they thought they would. In their vision, they thought surely within three years their congregation of thirty would be three hundred. But as they stand before their congregation of still thirty, they begin losing hope. They wonder why God has not moved in a mightier way. Looking now at their numbers, they decide it is time to call it quits.

Rather than taking this faithful congregation of thirty that has stuck with them for three years, getting on their faces before God, and asking His direction, these ministers have lost their perseverance, and they close the doors of the church.

Around the corner from that church is the church of the **"Proud Spirit"**:

This church began, centered right in the heart of God. A foundation of prayer was laid, and faith moved this house forward. The pastor stayed on his face before God and worked tirelessly and diligently to make certain everything was right in step with God's order. The church quickly began growing, and the pastor stood amazed at what *he* and God together had done. Programs began being implemented to please the people. Next, the dedicated praise and worship team was exchanged for a more professional sound. Soon, the leadership looked upon another ministry to build as they had first built, and before long, the world's standards had crossed the threshold of God's House.

The pastor's need for glory consumed the sanctuary, replacing God's glory – and finally, the proud spirit replaced God's Holy Spirit. The leaders became dictators rather than servants – and the people's love waxed cold.

Down the road from that church abides the church of the **"Fearful Spirit"**:

This is probably the saddest of all sanctuaries. For this church was built on love, centered in Christ, saturated in prayer, and persevered year after year, anxiously awaiting what God would do with divine expectation.

Then, God began moving. Suddenly, after all this time, family after family came – ushered in by the Holy Spirit. Ministries came forth, and the seats were filled. The pastor and leadership, moving forward in faith, began seeking for property that would become the "resting place" God intended. Plans were drawn, properties located, and prices procured.

Soon, something began happening. The leadership turned from the anticipated property to the status of the congregation. Their eyes focusing on what is, rather than what shall be, their faith began to fade. Before long, logic replaced faith, and doubt consumed the very center of this ministry. As their faith became contaminated by fear, it spread to their people. Seeping from the leadership and filling the congregation, they began doubting God's ability and His promise given. Even seasoned Christians weakened as the opposite of faith infiltrated their minds and hearts, and the Holy Spirit was smothered out by the spirit of fear.

Today, many years later, the church of the Fearful Spirit remains at its same location – with the same few families, and no vision of that which God had once intended it to be.

Oh, but brothers and sisters hold on for a moment. We are now crossing over the tracks. It's coming into view, there in the distance is the church of the "**Holy Spirit**":

This is the church everyone is talking about. It's amazing. Folks are coming from all over to check out what's going on here. I see one of the members walking to his car right now. Let me see if he can give us a glimpse of what has taken place in this house today.

"Sir, could you please tell me what it was that drew you to this house of worship?"

"Oh, praise God. There is really no way to explain it. I mean, it's the most phenomenal thing I've ever experienced. I came to this church two years ago. I'd attended church most all my life and went faithfully every service; but I met a guy at work one day that, well at the time, I thought he was a strange fellow. He was always happy, never down in the dumps; and even when his wife collapsed with a heart attack and had to be rushed to the hospital, Joe just gathered his things, got down on his knees, and said he was leaving her in God's hands and knew everything would be okay.

"It really started shaking me up because, quite frankly, I saw something in his life that I didn't have, and I was a Christian too. I knew I didn't have that same, what can I call it, victory and zeal that I saw in Joe's life. So, when his wife recovered and he returned to work, I asked him what religion he was. The answer he gave blew me away."

"You can't leave us hanging, friend. Please, go on. We have to know what he said that apparently made such an impact on you."

"Well, he gave a sheepish grin and patted me on the shoulder. Then he looked deep into my eyes and said, 'Russell, I don't have a religion; I have a relationship with my Heavenly Father. It doesn't matter where you go to church or what denomination you profess to be, it's what's going on in here,' and he pointed to my heart. He told me that is what's going to determine where you spend eternity. For wherever your heart is, that's where your treasure lies."

"Wow. That was pretty profound."

"Yeah, and after he told me that, he took time to share some of the promises God has given us in the Bible and who we really are in Christ. Once my eyes were opened to who I am in Christ, my whole life changed! I should tell you, I could no longer go to the church I'd been in all my life. Suddenly, I realized there was no power there. I wasn't being spiritually fed, and I knew I could not stay. It broke my heart because I loved those people, but when I tried talking to them about this new relationship I'd found and my desire to grow in God, they acted like I had just stepped off the deep end. One lady told me to be careful or I may become a *fanatic*. But when I study God's Word, I see that loving Jesus and desiring to give Him my all doesn't make me a fanatic. It simply makes me more like Him—Christ-like. So, longing to represent Him, I came here to visit, at the church of the Holy Spirit. And once I got a taste of what was going on, I couldn't leave!"

"That's great. So, tell us briefly, what was your service like today?"

"Indescribable! Immediately, upon entering His House, we felt His glorious presence, because of the prayers that are continually lifted by these believers. As we entered into praise and worship, God met with us. It was so exciting. Just before service began, a lady gave a praise report of what God had done. During last week's service, she went up for prayer. She had been diagnosed with cancer and would go this week to begin treatments. But after prayer last

70

week, she said she began feeling much better. When she went for her treatment, they did the prep tests, which were just formality, but something had happened that they could not explain. So, they tested her two more times. Finally, they broke the news to her. They could no longer find any cancer. No treatments were needed, and they said they had no explanation of what had happened. But she did! She was healed – and went home cancer-free!

"We never know what to expect when we come together. We just let God be God and do whatever is on His heart. We don't go by a bulletin; we just go with His flow!

"After praise and worship, our pastor spoke what could have only come from the heart of God. For you see, every sermon is fresh manna. He doesn't keep a file cabinet with sermon notes to draw from. Our pastor enters his prayer closet and gets straight from the heart of God what the people need. My pastor's not a hot-shot; he too is just in love with Jesus."

"Tell me, has this church experienced any splits? I mean, how can you possibly make everyone love each other and keep strife and division out as growth takes place?"

"Oh, you don't have to worry about that here. We give the Holy Spirit complete control to dissolve all issues. If anyone has aught against another, they go to them in love and work it out. If help is needed in resolving the matter, they meet with our elders and then the pastor if necessary, and together they pray and seek God's truth. Once you

71

put strife under the blood of Jesus, forgiveness flows forth, and you can once again fellowship in true agape love – the 'God-kind' of love.

"One last thing you will probably want to know as well. We don't have church cliques either. See, when the Holy Spirit reigns, everyone loves everyone as one big family, and we are growing every week. The bigger we get, the more we pray and seek God's face for His wisdom. It's wonderful – we wouldn't have it any other way!"

"Before we go, would you please tell me the address for this glorious church so I can share it with those reading this book? They too may want to visit. How can they get here?"

"Sure–it's easy. The address for this church is 2 Chronicles 7:14. And here is the most awesome part of all. Any church can become this church of the Holy Spirit. All they must do is enter into their prayer closet and determine to make their house a house of prayer, the way God intended it to be. Then, step aside and let all the glory go to God."

"What can they expect once they do this?"

"Oh brother, roll up your Holy Ghost jeans and prepare to swim. Once you give the Lord complete control, your church will be so full of love and the presence of God's glory, you'll be swimming in all the blessings God has for you. So much so, you'll have to go find others to share it all with! That is how God works!"

And *that* will conclude our glimpse into the church of the Holy Spirit.

Before leaving this chapter, however, may I ask you brothers and sisters in Christ: which church are you attending?

God has a perfect plan for your life. You must attend a house of worship where you can be fed and grow spiritually. Find that place that will help in reaching your full God-given potential to become *all* Christ destined you to be.

You will not find a perfect church, for church is filled with people. There will be imperfections, but it is the heart of the church that matters to God. Don't settle for mediocre. And most importantly, don't expect your church and your pastor to seek God's heart for you. You must enter His presence, fully humbling yourself and seeking Him. Then, join your brothers and sisters corporately in doing the same.

You will not find a perfect church, for church is filled with people. There will be imperfections, but it is the heart of the church that matters to God. Don't settle for mediocre.

You can rest assured the church that prays together, stays together. Man must step aside and give full reign to the leading of the Holy Spirit. Why? This will allow God's presence to fill His House and your heart and will give you His strength and power to carry with you, to give to all those you meet throughout the week . . . all for the glory of God!

STUDY GUIDE

⚞ Chapter 3 ⚟

SO, WHO AM I?

01) As you stand in front of your "spiritual" mirror right now and take a sincere look at yourself, what do you see? Who are you in Christ Jesus?

02) Who does God see when He looks down upon your heart as He did with King David?

03) Would God declare you to be a man/woman after *His* own heart? Why or why not?

04) Do you feel the Holy Spirit's nudge right now to lay down some things that may be keeping you from experiencing God's daily presence in your life? List them below:

05) What talents or gifts do you possess that you can offer to Christ? Have you dedicated those things to Him, or will you do so for His kingdom's use?

06) Perhaps you are one of those believers who has said, "I would gladly give God my gifts and talents – if I had any." Sound familiar? Great! You are a prime candidate to be used for God's glory. Are you willing to allow Him to use you? I mean *really* use you. Or are you hiding behind excuses of inability?

Quote Jeremiah 29:11, replacing the word "you" with your name.

Do you believe what God is saying to you in this passage? Do you *really* believe it? Are you ready to sincerely ask the Lord to show you what His plans for your life are? Will you obey when He shows you those plans for His glory?

07) Which of the churches named in this chapter represent your church?

Is the Holy Spirit welcome in your house of fellowship?

Is He welcomed in your heart?

Father, thank You for a fresh new day to serve You! From this day forward, I choose to put You first in my life in a greater measure than ever before. Right now, I choose to lay everything that I am, or ever hope to be, at your feet, Lord Jesus.

I read in Jeremiah 29:11 that You, the creator of Heaven and earth, have big plans for my life. Right now, I can't see or even begin to understand what Your perfect plan is Lord, but I trust You. And I choose, beginning now, to seek Your face daily in my prayer closet (Your storehouse) humbly asking, in faith, believing that You reveal those plans to me.

You said if I would earnestly ask I would receive. You also said You withhold no good thing from those who ask. Lord, I believe. Help my unbelief as I fully learn to rely on You. I trust in You and cleave to Your promises.

Help me to not only seek Your face for my life, but for the life of Your Church as well. Also, my nation, the United States of America, needs You, God, more than ever before. So many have turned from You and no longer regard Your name as holy. Many have taken Your principles and precepts and watered down Your Holy Word. They now call everything acceptable, but You have not changed Your mind. Give me, as Your child and representative of Heaven, Your heart to see the Church as You see the Church and Your boldness to say right is right and wrong is still wrong.

Lastly, I lift my house of fellowship to You, Father. Help me to pray daily for my pastor and leadership. Teach me how to be a true intercessor, and help me to never be guilty of gossiping or murmuring about this house You have placed me in. If things are not right, give me boldness to stand for Your truth, with no regard to consequences.

Thank you Lord for the plans You have for my life. Show me Your way and lead me in Your truth everlasting. I pray in the mighty name of Jesus - and all for Your glory!

Amen.

❧ Chapter 4 ❧

OUR HEAVENLY DNA

We are born, having a unique quality within us that is present from the time of conception. It is so distinct no one can deny its existence. It offers undeniable proof as to whom we belong, and screams out each time it is tested, "I belong to you Mom. I belong to you Dad." This quality is our DNA.

As born-again believers, we have the unique heavenly DNA of God. We have been re-born from above. Just as man was created with half his mother's DNA and half his father's DNA, God has placed within each re-born child of God His heavenly DNA.

To fully comprehend all God has done, we must have an understanding as to what DNA is. DNA, or deoxyribonucleic acid, is the material present in nearly all living organisms and is the carrier of genetic information.

According to the online dictionary *Lexico*, the word *genetic* relates to genes or heredity. The very word *genetic* originated from the word *genesis*, which means the origin, or formation of something. The word *Genesis* is derived from a Greek word meaning to be born or produced. The word *heredity* means the passing on of physical or mental characteristics genetically from one generation to another. It can also mean the inheritance of a title, office, or right. The origin of the word *heredity* comes from a Latin word meaning *heir* (Lexico, 2019)

As this is a summation of DNA in the natural, I believe it also describes our DNA in the supernatural.

As we learned in school from an early age, we are made up of twenty-three chromosomes from our father and twenty-three from our mother, bringing a perfect balance to a new life formed. If this new life had only the father's chromosomes and nothing more, it would equal death. Likewise, if this life contained the mother's chromosomes alone, again death would result. It is the bringing together of these chromosomes, half and half, that equals life.

In the beginning of time, God created man in His own image and breathed into (or filled) man with Himself. God then took man's rib and formed woman, again breathing into (or filling her) with His very life. They were born there-fore possessing Heaven's DNA: God's total perfection, or balance of God and man.

Man's life revolved around God's Spirit. He was filled with God's senses, God's fragrance, and he knew the voice of His Heavenly Father as He came to walk with him daily. What took place biologically within man's fleshly body to keep him functioning was probably given no thought. The things of God were his focus. Everything in his life cen-tered on his spirit man and fellowship with His Heavenly

Father. Until one day, Satan came to destroy this perfect union. He offered man that which he knew would alter the balance and allow sickness and death to enter.

According to information provided by the University of Utah's Genetic Science Learning Center, if an extra chromosome is present in our physical bodies, it distorts and causes a genetic disorder. Similarly, we find in the Bible, that anything added into our spirit, by man, will distort–causing a condition known as carnality. And just as we learn from the article "Extra or Missing Chromosomes," a genetic disorder caused by chromosomal abnormalities in a physical body limits the developmental stages and health of a person's life. Likewise, we learn from studying God's Holy Word that a carnal man will never walk in the fullness of who God intended him to be. He can never achieve all that God purposed for his life because his spiritual comprehension is blocked (Learn Genetics, 2019).

After the fall of man in the Garden of Eden, God saw the state of humanity, but He did not leave man there. Out of a love so great and so incomprehensible, our loving Father made a way to once again perfect the balance. He delivered the infallible cure.

"For God so loved the world that He gave His only begotten Son, that whoever believes in Him should not perish but have everlasting life" (John 3:16).

Jesus is the ultimate cure. It cost God the Father the life of His only son. All who will accept Jesus as their Lord and

Savior will receive God's genes, and God's heredity will be passed down to whosoever will. This heredity means we once again live a life filled with Heaven's perfect balance. Having Heaven's DNA breathed into our very being, we now live our life in Christ. Glorious, isn't it!

Sadly however, many believers do not realize who they are in Christ Jesus. Many have proclaimed Christ as Savior and Redeemer, yet they perceive things in the spirit as "mystical" or a "Hollywood" fantasy. They do not realize that when they were born-from-above, they were recreated into that "God-image" originally designed in the garden. With their Heavenly DNA restored, their spirit man now takes precedence over the natural.

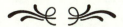

Your spirit is more real than your flesh. However, because you occupy the flesh, tangibly seeing, touching, and hearing with natural senses, you can become dull to your spirit man if you do not live life led by the Holy Spirit.

You may be saying, "Okay, this all sounds wonderful, but does every born-again believer automatically receive Heaven's DNA?" Yes, everyone who has truly accepted

Jesus as his Savior, turned from the old life, and has become that new, born-again creation. Anything other than that is a chameleon—someone acting like a Christian, having the very appearance of a Christian, but never having truly experienced new birth.

The worst thing the Church has ever done since its birth was to give people a false hope in their salvation, allowing them to live like the world without the Church holding them accountable. When we see a brother or sister in Christ stumble or drift into sin, it is our God-given responsibility to go to them in love and warn them. Be clear; be bold. But be filled with love when you must say, "You are living in sin; you can't live that way and be a child of God. Darkness cannot live in the light."

Far too many have walked down the aisle, said a little prayer, and left with absolutely no change in their lives, thinking they will end up in Heaven one day. However, without salvation, that new-birth from above, they are destined for hell, and sadly, the Church has often blessed them in their walk there.

The Church of the living God, the Bride of Christ, that One our Lord is soon returning to receive, is a people filled with His Heavenly DNA. They walk like their Father, talk like their Father, and have His eyes and His heart. They are led by His loving Holy Spirit. There has been a total transformation in their lives which began with conviction of sin and true repentance before God.

Christ warned in Matthew 7:21, "Not everyone who says to Me, 'Lord, Lord' shall enter the kingdom of heaven ..." Chapter three covered the components of how you would know, truly know, you have been saved. As you study Heaven's DNA, ask yourself, "How can I be sure I possess Heaven's DNA?"

Examine your fruit: Do you stand for Godly principles? Are you passionately praying for life instead of death? Do you believe your destiny on earth is not finished until you breathe your last breath? Do you believe you must come through the blood of Jesus to be saved? Do you believe one must live according to *all* the precepts and principles in God's Word, without picking and choosing only those you like? These are some of the traits that are characteristic in the DNA of God.

Salvation is a gift given by God. Your walk with Him is not meant to be complicated. There is much understanding to gain, and you will learn His principles and precepts by doing that which His Word declares, "Be diligent to present yourself approved to God, a worker who does not need to be ashamed, rightly dividing the word of truth" (2 Tim. 2:15).

A born-again child of God, recreated with Heaven's DNA, equals a life that is forever changed. He is now one with his Heavenly father.

> I am praying not only for these disciples
> but also for all who will ever believe in me

83

because of their testimony. My prayer for all
of them is that they will be one, just as you
and I are one, Father – that just as you are
in me and I am in you, so they will be in
us, and the world will believe you sent me. I
have given them the glory you gave me, so
that they may be one, as we are – I in them
and you in me, all being perfected into one.
(John 17:20-23 NLT)

You become one with God through Christ Jesus. God –
resting on man – a supernatural connection— life forever
changed. Even when life throws things at the born-again
believer, and he stumbles for a while, perhaps even stating,
"That's it. I can't do this anymore. I'm walking away; I'm cutting myself off from the family." It is at that crucial moment
the chameleon will be separated from the true child of
God. How? You can't divorce DNA. It is there to stay. Once
God has entered into your life, and you *know* Him and
have tasted of His mercy and His goodness, if you then
choose to pull your life away from Him, you are ripping or
tearing His Holy Presence and Spirit from your very being.
This, my friend, according to His Holy Scripture, equals an
eternal separation from God.

For it is impossible to restore to repentance
those who were once enlightened – those
who have experienced the good things of
Heaven and shared in the Holy Spirit, who
have tasted the goodness of the word of God
and the power of the age to come – and who

then turn away from God. It is impossible to bring such people to repentance again because they are nailing the Son of God to the cross again by rejecting Him, holding Him up to public shame. (Heb. 6:4-6 NLT)

You may walk away from your Heavenly Father for a season, but there will always be a wooing of the Holy Spirit to the true child of God.

You may walk away from your Heavenly Father for a season, but there will always be a wooing of the Holy Spirit to the true child of God. It is at those times it is extremely important to understand a second principle concerning your chemistry: environment.

In addition to the DNA acquired from biological parents that form the way you look, your likes and dislikes, and influences your personality traits, you are also altered to a large extent by the environment in which you live. Many children, having grown up in an abusive environment or broken home, will spend years in counseling of some type to try overcoming the harmful effects of that negative environment which held them captive. Tragically, some never escape the bondage of those chains.

As a reborn child of God, you too can be altered by the spiritual environment you allow yourself to live in. An environment lacking in faith, love, truth, and fellowship with the Holy Spirit and with others can keep you from living the God-kind of life (or zoë life) God intended.

Learning to live in His presence and be guided by His Spirit does not require vast intellect, but rather a passion and hunger that cannot be filled. Years ago, while working in youth ministry, I would talk with people and could tell just by talking with them if they were really saved. Some were in leadership, yet I knew they had never experienced true salvation. How did I know? Our spirits never communed.

While talking with one individual, I began sharing the things of God. As I spoke, she stared as though I had a third eye in the middle of my head – I knew she had a learned religion rather than a relationship with a Living God.

Some people get wrapped up in the social aspect of church and religion and mistake it for true salvation. When you encounter God, there is passion. DNA has with it the passion of Heaven. When people have no passion at all, when there is not anything in God that stirs an emotion, something is wrong. They have either grown carnal, or they're lost.

Please don't misunderstand. I am not saying your salvation is contingent upon emotions and feelings. It is true we live by faith, and everyone processes his or her experiences differently. However, there is no way possible for man to have a true encounter with God and not feel His emotion.

Have you ever watched a baby being birthed? When a baby comes forth from its mother's womb, it cries. Something within that baby is made to cry out as it is born into this worldly realm and breathes on its own for the first time. That baby cries out because it knows there has been a forever change.

That is the way it is when you get saved. You are like a baby that has just been birthed. You take a deep breath, breathing in the breath of Heaven. It is at that very moment you receive Heaven's DNA. You are born into what Heaven gave you–the very destiny God purposed and designed for your life even before you were naturally born. God's Word states in Jer. 1:5 that He knew you before you were in your mother's womb, and He called and appointed you.

Christ spoke those words over every man, woman, boy, and girl who ever has or ever will accept Him. Do you realize when you repented of your sin, believed in the Lord Jesus Christ, and accepted Him as Lord and Savior, you walked out of the carnal realm and into the realm of Heaven?

While working on the conclusion of this chapter, I was perplexed as to the totality of what the Holy Spirit wanted to convey regarding *being* that new creation in Christ. Nothing was placed in this book without much prayer, study, research, and confirmation from God. Yet, I knew the chapter could not end by merely stating we step into this new realm. There was something more. But what, Lord? After much time spent combing through all that had been written regarding our heavenly DNA, the "born-again" encounter with God, and then the birthing into our new destiny, suddenly the Lord spoke forth Hebrews Chapter Four.

I've heard many sermons preached from the third chapter of Hebrews, sermons that talk about the rest the Lord will give you from your troublesome load (Heb. 3:4). I have also heard preachers preach from the fourth chapter of Hebrews on the promised rest from God that we have been given, yet many never expound on it further (Heb. 4:1-10). But that day as I was researching, humbled and listening, the Holy Spirit taught regarding this blessed rest and what it means to all born-again believers.

In the third chapter of Hebrews, we read of the children of Israel and their disobedience and refusal to believe God. In verses 16-19, we read of how they heard God's voice, sinned (through disobedience and rebellion), and died in the wilderness. Verse 19 declares, "So we see that they could not enter in, because of unbelief."

Then, we go onto the fourth chapter of Hebrews:

> God's promise of entering His place of rest
> still stands, so we ought to tremble with fear
> that some of you might fail to get there. For
> this Good News – that God has prepared
> a place of rest – has been announced to

us just as it was to them. But it did them no good because they didn't believe what God told them. For only we who believe can enter his <u>place of rest</u>. As for those who didn't believe, God said "In my anger I made a vow: They will never enter my place of rest," even though His place of rest has been ready since He made the world. (Heb. 4:1-3 NLT)

So God's rest is there for people to enter. But those who formerly heard the Good News failed to enter because they disobeyed God. So God set another time for entering His <u>place of rest</u>, and that time is today. God announced this through David a long time later in the words already quoted: "Today you must listen to His voice. Don't harden your hearts against Him." This new place of rest was not the land of Canaan, where Joshua led them. If it had been, God would not have spoken later about another day of rest. So, there is a <u>special rest</u> *still waiting* for the people of God. For all who enter into God's rest will find rest from their labors, just as God rested after creating the world. Let us do our best to enter that <u>place of rest</u>. For anyone who disobeys God, as the people of Israel did, will fall. For the Word of God is full of living power. It is sharper than the sharpest knife, cutting deep into our

innermost thoughts and desires. It exposes
us for what we really are. (Heb. 4:6-12 NLT)

The word *rest* in these passages of scripture, when refer-
ring to the place of rest God has prepared for us to enter
into, is used in the context as a noun – not a verb. A place
– not an action.

Verse 10 declares, "For all who enter into <u>God's rest</u> will
find rest from their labors." You see, by entering into that
place of rest (noun), they will rest (verb) from their labors.

When we are birthed into our heavenly DNA and begin to
realize who we are in Christ, we also learn there is now a
special dwelling place prepared for us. Let me illustrate. In
the natural, when you place a coat upon your body – you
are in that coat and that coat is on you, covering you as
you abide within it. So it is also in the spirit. God covers
the lives of His children with Himself. He has that special
place of abode prepared. It has been prepared since the
foundation of the world; that's what His Word said in verse
3. He has been waiting for us to step in. That special, holy
dwelling of God Himself (the Holy Spirit) now covers our
life, as we abide in Him!

There is much for us to understand, proclaim, and walk in as born-again children of God. Our very beings are now made up of God's genes. Heaven's heredity has now been passed on to us. We are heirs of Christ Jesus and have now inherited all of who God is.

As Paul wrote in his Letter to the Ephesians, I pray for you:

> that the God of our Lord Jesus Christ, the Father of glory, may give to you the spirit of wisdom and revelation in the knowledge of Him, the eyes of your understanding being enlightened; that you may know what is the hope of His calling, what are the riches of the glory of His inheritance in the saints, and what is the exceeding greatness of His power toward us who believe, according to the working of His mighty power. (Eph.1:17-19)

May you understand who Christ has called you to be. May you see that *this* is the resting place God has for you. As God wraps Himself around your life, rest *in* Him as

He rests *on* you. As you learn to live your new life fully clothed in God Himself, you will enter into His rest. That place of "God on man," just as it began with Adam in the Garden of Eden.

May you wrap your life in God's Word, the textbook of your heavenly DNA, and live the destiny He fully intends. May you look more like your Father every day. May you walk as He walks and talk as He talks. May you have His heart and His eyes, as you press daily toward the mark of the high calling in Christ, to achieve *all* He has purposed and planned. May you *be* part of the overcoming, God-fearing, spirit-filled, power-packed, agape-loving, one-with-Christ, united, inseparable, body of believers Christ has called His Church to be . . . all for the glory of God!

STUDY GUIDE

~ Chapter 4 ~

HEAVEN'S DNA

01) In the beginning, God created man in His own image and breathed into him Heaven's DNA. This was God's perfect balance. As a born-again believer, I must understand that Heaven's DNA–the very essence of God–has been restored into my life.

The life I now live is no longer my own. Record Galatians 2:20 here:

_____

_____

_____

_____

_____

02) When man was first created, his life revolved around the presence of God. He was filled with God's senses, God's fragrance, and he knew the voice of his Heavenly Father when He came to walk with him daily.

Today, our Heavenly Father longs to have this same relationship with us. He has so much to speak into our lives, but many do not even know how to recognize His voice. We cannot carry the fragrance of our Heavenly Father until we first learn how to sense His presence and commune with Him – one on one.

How can we know our Father's voice? How can we sense His divine presence in our lives? It isn't complicated. It is achieved the very same way in the spirit realm as in the natural realm. If you are married, think for a moment of how your relationship developed:

First, you became familiar with that special someone. Perhaps you heard of him through a friend or met him in a hallway and your eyes locked. In whatever way you first met, something inside said, "I have to know you better," and you took measures to ensure that happened.

As you became closer, you longed to spend more time together. Whatever it took to get those fleeting moments of time–skipping lunch just to talk, waking up an hour early to say good morning before work, or even giving up precious television time (soap operas perhaps), if that's what it took for one more moment together.

In time, you knew you could no longer live without that special someone. You were now so tightly knit that others would smell his cologne on your clothes and know you had been together, for you were now carrying his very fragrance.

Then, the day came. The day you took that final step and said, "I do." Meaning, you knew you could no longer exist, nor did you desire to, as that person you had been. You knew there was a new life awaiting you that would forever change who you are—your name, your residence—and although you would have to give up things you possessed from your single days; you knew none of that mattered any more. You no longer desired to be merely who you had been.

You stepped in and took on the identity of the one you loved. From that day forward, no one ever saw you again as that single one you once were. You were always seen as "Mr. and Mrs. Someone Special" – and you smiled, because the two of you had become forever one.

Now, go back to the beginning of this story and replace that special someone with your Heavenly Father. Reread this as your salvation story, the day you met your precious *First Love.*

Taking the same measures in developing your relationship with Him is how you learn to recognize His voice, sense His presence, and carry His fragrance perpetually. Others will know when you have truly taken on His identity. They will no longer be able to separate you from the Christ you love, for you have become forever one!

Dear Heavenly Father,

Thank you for giving me Your life-changing DNA. I now realize my life is no longer my own — and I praise You for that marvelous truth! Enlighten my understanding in a greater measure than ever before. For Your Word is a lamp unto my feet and a light unto my path. Teach me how to truly hide Your Word in my heart that I may not sin against You but rather step into that God-given destiny You prepared for my life before I was even conceived.

Teach me how to enter into that perfect place of rest in You, "God on man." Help me learn how to wrap my life in You, guided by Your precious Holy Spirit, and clothed with the very essence of God. May I be inseparable from Your love, oh Lord.

Amen!

~≪ Chapter 5 ≫~

RISE TO THE CALL

'll never forget the day God brought inner-healing into my life. I felt so free and alive; it was as though I was inhaling fresh, clean air that came in through my nostrils and swept down into the very depths of my soul. I once again felt exactly as I did when I first received Christ as my Savior. However, this time it was not for my salvation, but rather for my total deliverance. I had come out of more than six years of the deadest, driest desert anyone could ever encounter. Just as the children of Israel knew their deliverer had come when they were freed from Egypt, I recognized the delivering hand of my Heavenly Father. I had so longed to feel His touch, to hear even His still small voice within, or that special tap once more at my heart's door.

As I began to feel His presence and experience the peace of His inner healing, He also placed a new desire within me – the call to enter a level in Him to which I'd never gone. This was God's mandate to *rise to Warrior Level,* and this mandate was not for me only. This is His call to all believers.

Rising to my feet, I knew I had received marching orders to "GO." I became so excited. I knew I was finally taking

97

my rightful place in Him as a *child of the King* – the status given to us upon entering His family. I felt as though I could conquer the world, holding the Savior's hand and marching forward. Then, I did what a soldier must never do on the battlefield. I began looking back—back through life's rear-view mirror while trying to move forward. I started apologizing to God, repenting and then living under condemnation.

Why had I allowed myself to get into that deep, dark valley in the first place? I was that teen who, along with my brothers, drove through the streets of Maryville, Tennessee, with the radio blasting the songs of the popular contemporary Christian artists of that day: The Imperials, Evie, and Dallas Holm and Praise. Stopping at every red light and shouting to other nearby cars the salvation of the Lord. We were in a time in America where gas shortages were being experienced, and in those days most everyone drove around with the windows down during nice weather, so we'd scream, "God loves you and there will NEVER be a shortage on HIS love!"

But now, as I looked back over my younger years and the way I openly and freely shared the message of God's love, my mind would flash back over the past six years. A cold, black cloud would form, and I'd say, "Lord, I am so very sorry. All that time I wasted. How many lives passed by during that period that I was supposed to touch?" Then I'd start feeling weaker, both physically and spiritually, and less worthy to be called His child.

I'd go back to church on Sunday and again be reminded of who I am in Christ, the authority He has given to me as a believer, and how I am to operate as a child of the King. I'm royalty (that's what Jesus called us). I'd feel strengthened as I left God's House and then, before reaching my house, here would come those reminders all over again. Everything I'd done wrong over the past, you know – six years–and I'd weep and mourn before God.

Until one day, God said, "Enough is enough!"

I was alone at home and once again found myself repenting before God. "Oh God, I am so sorry. I hope I still have enough time left in my life to accomplish what You'd have me do for You. I wasted all those years Lord and now…" and on I went. Suddenly, the Lord spoke to my heart: "Remember Joseph. He accomplished much for Me yet spent years in prison. I don't look upon those years of captivity – I want your *now*. Look at Esther and be wise, for I have created *you* for such a time as this!"

I will never forget those words. He knew how to get my attention, and He knew what had to take place for me to grow and mature into that acceptable child of God, fit for Kingdom use. I had to get my eyes off of *me* and begin focusing on advancing His Kingdom on earth, as it is in Heaven. If we will learn to recognize His voice and heed His instruction, He can then equip us with His perfect plan. However, if we go astray (whether it is through our own right, or an attack of the enemy), He patiently waits until our "wandering days" are over and we return to that place

He has prepared. As we then begin looking unto Him and positioning ourselves at His feet, He says "Are you ready now? Buckle up and hang on for the ride." And He drops His mandate deep into our heart and says, "Go!"

Many of you are asking that same question I asked, "Is there still enough time to complete that plan You had purposed for my life, Lord?"

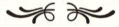

Remember Moses. Moses was a born leader. God chose him while he was still in his mother's womb. The devil knew it and made plans for Moses's life. A decree went forth that all male babies must die, but *someone* forgot to inform the devil that God always has a way of escape for His chosen ones. Moses went from a basket floating in the waters with no hope of survival, to a palace filled with all the riches of the kingdom.

Then, as Moses grew, God placed a mandate on his life. Moses knew he was to lead his people out of captivity, but he took God's matters into his own hands, and it ended in murder. Can you imagine how he must have felt as he fled the city and ran into the desert? He was called a leader, a deliverer of God's people, yet suddenly he was residing on the backside of a desert. He knew he could not return to the place God had called him. I can almost hear his cries of desperation as he set up camp in the desert for forty years: "Oh God, look at what I've done. You had a high calling on my life, and now, I have totally blown it. I know You will never be able to use me again Lord, and those thoughts and plans You had for me are probably over." Day after day, year after year, Moses contended in the desert wondering if he would ever experience God's presence or glory again. Then one day, as he walked along the sandy paths just as he'd walked for forty years, he came upon a bush. Something started tingling deep inside, and he stopped in his tracks. He hadn't felt *anything* for forty years.

"God?"

"Moses, take off your shoes."

"That bush, it's burning Lord, but it's not being consumed. I feel the tingling."

"Moses, take off your shoes for that ground which you are standing on is holy ground." (Exod. 3:1-5)

It was the Glory of God returning unto Moses. And you know the rest of the story (or if not, read it in Exodus 3). God's plan for Moses's life did not change. He just had to take Moses around the backside of the desert to burn all those things out of him that weren't God, so He could fill Moses with everything that was God.

And that day, alone in my home, God reminded me that it took Moses forty years before he completely surrendered every part of himself to the plan God purposed for his life. That day, Christ gently reminded me, we must all learn to count the cost in this new life in Christ Jesus. He also reminded me of men and women throughout scripture that accomplished great things for His Kingdom – they too experienced "down times" in the Lord. He then said, "Now, take my marching orders (or revelation of who I am) and go – the harvest awaits you!"

As I heard His voice, everything within me leapt for joy. Excitement filled my being, and I felt as the prophet Jeremiah must have felt as he sprang forth, deciding to do His Lord's command. He couldn't contain the joy of the Lord any longer. As he jumped up, he proclaimed it was like fire shut up in his bones! (Jer. 20:9) The feeling of a child set free . . . a Christian matured to Warrior Level. No longer looking back, but rather eyes fixed forward to what lies ahead. Equipped and anxious; ready to accomplish all God has in store.

Yes, God has a call for those choosing to step into their rightful position and pick up that mantle of authority God has prepared for them. His marching orders are ready. He is waiting for you to step forward and answer as Isaiah did: "Here am I Lord, send me" (Isa. 6:8).

He has a special place prepared for you – in His Harvest Field. Matthew 9:37-38 reads: "Then He said to His disciples, 'The harvest truly is plentiful, but the laborers are few. Therefore pray the Lord of the harvest to send out laborers into His harvest.'"

Will you position yourself, oh Warrior? Will you accept the challenge? Are you ready for a life that will be forever changed, at a level in which you have never walked? Are you ready for a taste of God's goodness, so sweet nothing on earth could ever compare? Are you ready for waters so deep you will no longer wade in His mercy but rather swim in His grace?

Most importantly, do you truly understand who you are in Christ? I know we've talked about the Heavenly DNA we possess, but we must also learn how to live and enjoy *all* Christ has given to us.

You can be the child of the wealthiest man in town, live in the finest home, and have millions of dollars in the bank, but if all you do is sit in your bedroom and say, "I am a member of the wealthiest, most well-renowned family," yet never leave that small, enclosed room to walk among the people or use your debit card to redeem all that is available to you, that abundant, beautiful treasure your father has so lovingly bestowed upon you, means absolutely nothing. You can one day die with untold riches stored up in a vault – completely untouched.

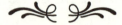

You must live the life of a blessed child. Walk the walk and talk the talk; invest your time learning how to use and care for that which has been given unto you.

You must live the life of a blessed child. Walk the walk and talk the talk; invest your time learning how to use and care for that which has been given unto you. It is a growing process, for if you haphazardly care for your wealth, much will be lost or stolen from you, without your ever even realizing it is gone.

You'll end up in poor investments which quickly drain you of your stored treasure. Placing your trust in the hands of those who are not looking out for your best interest will rob you unjustly, and not listening to those with sound advice who have knowledge in caring for your assets, can bankrupt your entire estate.

So it is in the spiritual realm, my friend. You have been reborn into a royal family. All that your Heavenly Father *is* and *possesses* is yours. What will you do with the riches of His glory He so longs to bestow upon your life? There was once a Christian radio station in our area that had a glorious saying they often played. "What God gives is His gift to you. What you become is your gift to God."

You have your marching orders–God's precious Word. Devour it daily. Follow Paul's instruction to Timothy: Study to show yourself approved unto God as that workman who need not be ashamed, rightly dividing the Word of Truth (2 Tim. 2:15). Pick up that rod of authority God has given you as a passionate believer. Read the book of Ephesians and know who you are in Christ. Study it, mark it, recite it, and proclaim it. *It is yours* – All of it! And now, being equipped with the whole armor of God, take hold and walk in the gifts and calling Christ has given unto you, oh Warrior. You are now ready.

Go forth and rise to the call . . . all for the glory of God!

STUDY GUIDE

≈ *Chapter 5* ≈

RISE TO THE CALL

01) Sadly, many Christians spend years of their lives looking back at past failures and defeat. By remaining captive to *yesterday*, countless millions will miss out on the glorious treasures God has stored in their *now*.

Where do you stand with your "marching orders" today? Are you actively pursuing the gifts and calling Christ has placed within you? Take a moment and ask the Lord if there are things in your life that are holding you captive to your past. As the Holy Spirit reveals them to you, write them down:

_____

_____

_____

02) The story given in this chapter told of the child of a wealthy man. There is a spiritual contrast, examine and make certain you are not falling prey to the enemy's trap.

- **Poor investments can quickly drain you of stored treasures:**

In the natural, you can place your money in faulty stocks or new ventures that go sour. So it is in the spirit. Be careful where you sow the funds God has entrusted to you. The Bible warns to "know those who labor among you" (1 Thess. 5:12) and ". . . you will reap what you sow" (Gal. 6:7 and 2 Cor. 9:6).

If you sow your offerings (and even worse – tithes) into ministries that are not following God's leading or into those ministries whose leadership is living in disobedience before God, you are doing the same with God's money as if you tossed it to the wind (Hosea 8:7). It will do no one any good, and you will reap from whatever is the bounty of that ministry–good or bad!

- **Placing your trust in the hands of those who are not looking out for your best interest can rob you unjustly:**

Christ has called us to be good stewards of God's money. He gave the parable of the talents and the unwise steward as an example of what happens when we do not wisely use the gifts and talents we have been blessed with. Furthermore, when we haphazardly give God's money away without first making it a matter of prayer, often we can place money into the hands of those with evil intent. In so doing, your good deed has done nothing but leave "holes in your pockets" (Hag. 1:6 NLT). The more money you make, the further in debt you become. Suddenly you will ask, "Why is it that I can never get ahead?" God's hand cannot bless that which goes against His Word and principles. However, when we wisely use the money, gifts, and talents He has entrusted into our care, the hand of God will actually bless us with many benefits other than monetary gain alone. Good health, debts paid off, businesses prospering, and promotions at work are a few that come to mind.

- **Not listening to those with knowledge of how to care for your assets can bankrupt your entire estate!**

   The Bible tells us to always seek wise counsel (Prov. 11:14). Listening to everyone and doing as others do is a dangerous place to live. Each of us have a unique set of circumstances, and God alone knows what lies ahead. Pray for direction in the choices you make. Seek counsel from those whom you know listen to God and have a proven track record of godly success (a life totally surrendered and prospering).

03) In question one, you wrote down those things that have held you captive to your past. Let's conclude this chapter by pressing toward the mark of the high calling in Christ, as we read in Philippians 3:14. Examine every area of your life right now and ask, "Lord, what are the gifts You have placed within my life?" What is it deep within your heart you most desire to do? Are obstacles in your way?

Often, we suppress those God-given gifts and callings because we feel too inadequate to fulfill them or think that dream is way too big. May I remind you, your Heavenly Father is lacking for *nothing*. A dream or desire too big for you is a perfect way to know it must be God! Surrender all to Him and walk in that calling He has destined for your life.

Be bold. Write down the deepest, sincerest desires that are upon your heart. *All* you want and dream of accomplishing for God:

_____

_____

_____

_____

Now, join with me in believing that the God you serve is well able to do "exceedingly, abundantly above all that we ask or think…" (Eph. 3:20).

Will you surrender your life *totally* to His loving care?

Dear Heavenly Father,

Thank you for teaching me how to rise to the call. I know I must count the cost daily and surrender myself fully unto You. I choose, from this day forward, to do that very thing. Help me Lord to never look back at those things in my past which have held me captive but instead look ahead to a future filled with Your blessings.

Take my hand, Father, as I step out in faith to begin walking in the gifts and calling You have placed within. Remind me of those desires that are buried deep within my heart - those things I thought were too big to ever really materialize. I repent for not trusting You, Lord.

I now realize every desire You place within me is there by divine conception, and if I will place my life totally in Your hands, You will give me the very desires of my heart, for they will be Your desires too.

I accept my "marching orders" this day. Help me to be that mighty warrior You have called me to be. Help me to stand strong, knowing You are always with me. Thank you for counting me worthy of the high calling of Christ.

May I forever go when You say, "Go".

In Jesus's mighty name,

Amen!

❧ Super Christian ❧

As I sat in church on Sunday, I looked out into the crowd. "Oh, there's a Super Christian, Lord; I know she makes You proud.

"She helps with all the children, does her best to teach them right, and they know she is available should they need her day or night.

"Every church fundraiser, no need to ask if she'll be there. You know you can always count on her, even if others do not care.

"And when the ladies meet for a special time together, this sister will be there, regardless of the weather. And when our church revivals come, I never ask if she'll attend. She's one sister I just know, on whom I can depend."

Then as the service started, pastor asked we all come kneel. I couldn't sit this one out for God's presence was so real. As I got down on my knees, at first I did not see, but the little Super Christian knelt down right beside of me.

I listened so intently, wondering what eloquent words she'd say, for I had no idea how a Super Christian would even pray.

"Oh God, please help me," was her cry, "to make it through another day. I don't want to let You down — please help me Lord, I pray. Sometimes my strength grows weary, and I feel so all alone. Please help me to remember it is Your strength that keeps me strong."

Oh no, I thought. Oh Jesus, you've got to help this sister make it through. Without her doing all she does,

I don't know what this church would do! Oh help her Lord; please give her the strength she needs now to survive. For without her going and doing and being, this church surely could not thrive.

The Lord then so gently spoke, "My child, I hear your prayer. But it is for such a time as this that I have placed you there. This one you call Super Christian, when I look down I see my loving, caring servant who just gives her all to Me.

"She cares for youth and children, who without a leader would not know what to do. She helps with the fundraisers when no one else will see them through. She attends the ladies' meetings because these sisters are her 'family,' and regularly attending revivals draws her ever closer still to Me.

"And you, my child, have not by chance heard her heart's cry this day. For I have placed you by her side to ask this before you pray: Will you step up and take her hand and vow to do your part, to give your sister strength and share the burden of her heart? Will you fill in where there's a need and seek My face and intercede? Will you my child, will you?" I heard my Savior gently plead.

I then began to feel the tears run quickly down my face. "Yes Lord, I will. I vow this day to step up and take my place."

As I took my sister's hand, I gently whispered, "You are not alone." I asked the Lord to equip her with His strength to carry on. "And if the burden gets too great, just call me day or night and place it upon my shoulders for two will put ten thousand out to flight!"

Then as I left the altar, I looked out into the crowd.

There were no Super Christians. That is not what makes God proud.

He just wants willing servants who will give to Him their all and work together hand in hand to carry out His call. For He said within His Word, "If my people called by My name will humble themselves and pray, then I will hear from Heaven and will heal their land this day. (2 Chron. 7:14, paraphrased)"

There's so much work for us to do, no one can do it alone. We truly need each other and God's strength to carry on. No, God doesn't need Super Christians, that is clear to see, just servants who really love Him. He so longs for you and me!

≈ Chapter 6 ≈

GO! WITH CARE

" **G**o." That is the mandate given by God to all His passionate, fire-filled believers. Yet tragically, many Christians take off running with their marching orders and leave the one mandate behind which is essential in being an effective warrior.

I once heard a story of two servants who were given an important message to deliver to the King. One, full of zeal and determining to arrive first, took off with great haste. However, he left so quickly that he forgot the written message he was to present and proclaim. Upon his arrival he stood before the King exhausted, wearied from the journey, and empty-handed. With great fury the King cast the servant out and awaited the approaching servant's arrival. That one came prepared, and his voice was heard as he proclaimed a message of deliverance.

This story sets an example for all Christians. Please take heed. When we, as born-again believers, begin our walk with God, or take off, we must be very careful to make certain we are walking in our Father's footsteps. If we fail to walk in His steps, we may find ourselves stomping others along the pathway, often not even realizing we are doing so.

The anxious servant was full of zeal but lacked revelation. Taking off in his own might, may have appeared as though he were running his race with excellence, far ahead of the other servant. Yet arriving at his destination, he had no voice. If we, being filled with zeal alone, set out on our own, we will end up doing one of two things upon reaching those God has set in our path: either we will try telling them God loves them, but have only empty words, or we will beat them up by badgering them with what *we think* God wants to say, without having His heart to proclaim.

It is crucial as we begin fulfilling our call in ministry that we allow ourselves time to sit under a pastor or mentor who will walk alongside us and teach us servant leadership. The Bible warns against novices being placed in leadership positions without the proper ministry covering or equipping by those seasoned (1 Tim. 3:6). Perhaps that is why so many experience hurt in the Church today. Perhaps that is why many come to the House of God seeking refuge and help, but instead find hurt and despair. Too often Christians are like the servant that merely went, leaving behind his lord's message of deliverance, and the Father's heart of compassion.

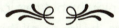

It is crucial as we begin fulfilling our call in ministry that we allow ourselves time to sit under a pastor or mentor who will walk alongside us and teach us servant leadership.

Our journey is the lives of those God places in our daily path; and He HAS a message for them—one which He wants to convey through us, His servants.

Be careful my brothers and sisters in Christ. *Be very careful.* This gospel message must go forth. But we must endeavor to be that servant God can use to change lives and make a difference for His Kingdom. Exactly what is the message to be delivered? What could possibly be so powerful that it brings hope and healing, life and liberty, yet so detrimental that without it we will cause deep hurt, confusion, and chaos to abound?

Let's look in 1 Corinthians 13:

> Though I speak with the tongues of men and of angels, but have not love, I have become sounding brass or a clanging cymbal . . . love suffers long and is kind; Love does not envy; love does not parade itself, is not puffed up; does not behave rudely, does not seek its own, is not provoked, thinks no evil; does not rejoice in iniquity, but rejoices in the truth; bears all things, believes all things, hopes all things, endures all things. Love never fails . . . and now abide faith, hope, love… but the greatest of these is love. (1 Cor. 13:1, 4-8, 13)

I know upon stating this scripture, the immediate thought of some was, "Oh, I know this one." It's known to all Christians as the Love Chapter. All Christians *know* this chapter, yet

116

sadly far too few *live* this passage. Remember the commandments Jesus gave in Matthew 22:37-39: "Jesus said to him, You shall love the Lord your God with all your heart, with all your soul, and with all your mind. This is the first and great commandment. And the second is like it: You shall love your neighbor as yourself."

These are the greatest commandments of all. By example, Jesus taught if we would walk step-by-step, day-by-day, living and breathing these commandments, we would be accomplishing His Father's perfect will, fulfilling exactly what He commissioned for us as His children.

Why do you think these are the most important commandments? Making sure others get saved must surely be *the* most important task. If you die without salvation, you go to hell. Yes, that's true. That is why God sent His only son Jesus to come and die on the cross in our place, so we could obtain life everlasting. But Jesus didn't just jump down to earth as a man, go to all those not living right, and begin badgering them, proclaiming, "You know what your problem is? You have to get your heart right with my Father. You are worthless, and unless you repent from your wicked ways, you are going to hell!"

No. Jesus came to earth in the form of a newborn baby lying in a manger. A child of humble beginnings. He grew and learned as He walked through life, just as we do. Then He stepped into the calling that was placed upon Him and sought His Father's face, *daily*, to make sure every step He took was taken in love—agape love. The perfect

"God-kind" of love. And this is the ingredient that sets us apart from the world in which we live: "By this all will know that you are My disciples, if you have love for one another" (John 13:35).

Many are right now asking as they read this book, "That's great, but what about those who make it impossible to love them? Have you not encountered any of them?" Yes, we all have. And may I give you a shocking revelation? Those people are everywhere! No matter where you run to get away from them, they'll be there waiting for you.

How can I know this? Because people are imperfect and where there are people, there are problems. Take away people, you'll take away problems. But then who will you fellowship with? You'd only have yourself, and I hate to burst your bubble, but once you are alone with only you, you may find that not all the problems you encountered were "other people." Some could have actually involved a little (or a lot) of you in them.

Jesus knew it would not always be easy to love. What greater example could He have demonstrated than laying down His life at the hands of those who hated Him? He warned us before leaving earth that we would go through the same things; then He gave hope when He encouraged His followers to ". . . be of good cheer, I have overcome the world" John 16:33. That was His message to us. Can't you just hear Him today, "Don't worry believers. Don't wonder if you will be able to walk in love, for I *am* your example, and I conquered and overcame; so you too will conquer and overcome, if you walk as I have instructed you to walk – in my unconditional, everlasting, never-ending, merciful, forgiving, agape love."

After spending more than six years of living life void of love, refusing to reach out to others and refusing to allow others to reach in, may I tell you a fact first-hand? Life without love is not life at all. It's more like a walking death or mere existence. It is horrible, excruciating, and painful. Don't ever be responsible for causing someone to live that way. I don't care how much you may think you cannot stand them, they are not your enemy. Satan is your enemy. He is trying to get you, as a believer, in a place where bitterness and hatred will rule, so he may keep you positioned in defeat.

One thing we often fail to realize is if we are responsible for hurting others, we are contaminating our own spiritual blood with a toxic poison called bitterness. As that wounded brother or sister staggers through her life, trying to exist with that poison injected into her system, we too are operating out of a toxic life which will only produce hurt. There is only one antidote by which to rid this poison. It is called inner healing.

I will never forget a book I read at the age of nineteen. It was written by Charles Swindoll and was called *Strengthening Your Grip.* Reading this book was a prerequisite to attending a discipleship camp I participated in. To whomever the individual was that mandated the reading of that book, may I say, "God bless you!" That book changed my way of thinking as a young person and caused me to take my walk before God seriously. There was a poem by Leslie B. Flynn that was quoted in this book, and the lines, these many years later, I have never forgotten: "To dwell above with saints we love, that will be grace and glory. To live below with saints we know; that's another story!" (Swindoll 1982, 178).

You are not the first who has found it difficult at times to get along with brothers and sisters in Christ. Do you want to know a godly principle that will take you past the hurt and into miraculous healing that will last throughout your lifetime? The act of forgiveness. That means taking that one who comes to mind when you think of those who have hurt or wronged you, getting on your face before God, and asking Him to forgive you for the bitter feelings you have harbored. It means asking Him to remove that bitterness completely, severing the very root and plucking it from your heart. And lastly, it means going to that person and asking forgiveness as well. Yes, even if she were the one who hurt you. Remember, hurting people hurt people. Do you realize those who rose up against you, hurting you the deepest, are probably the very ones who most need God's love poured into their lives? Who better can God use to restore than the one they had victimized?

Do you realize those who rose up against you, hurting you the deepest, are probably the very ones who most need God's love poured into their lives? Who better can God use to restore than the one they had victimized?

I know many of you are probably thinking, "This sounds great, but what if I go to them and they won't receive me? What if I try and it backfires?"

But what if you go, and God brings complete restoration to their soul? What if you go as God has asked you to, and He uses you to bring them back to that place He has longed for them to return for years? *What if* the calling on their life is so great they become the next worldwide evangelist, and *you* are the torch God used to rekindle their flame?

If you go and they do not receive, you have fulfilled God's command to love, and He will honor your display of His affection. Going releases you from that place you have been held captive. You are now free to soar with God.

Remember early in this book I told you one of the deepest hurts I ever suffered was at the hand of a woman pastor? Well, there is another part to that story I have not yet shared. After everything had transpired and we left the church, it took a while for us to allow God's repositioning. When something happens that knocks you off your spiritual feet, it takes time to get your focus back and be able to once again hold your head high. You must get your mind back under subjection to the things of God. Failing to do this will lead only to further chaos and confusion.

It did take time for us to allow God's healing and have a desire to even consider reconciliation. I still remember the phone call we made, asking our former pastor and her husband if we could meet with them. We left a message because they would not answer our call. A few days later, her husband came to our home. We all spoke and agreed we were sorry for anything done or said that caused hurt, and each asked forgiveness one to the other. But our former pastor would not come. Her husband asked that we just give her time. He said she needed to heal before talking to anyone, and she was not at that place yet. He also said they were preparing to move to another state and would only be in this area for a short while, awaiting the sale of some property.

We never heard from them again that I can recollect; and life went on. However, several years later, I had a dream about my former pastor. I dreamed I drove to a house and parked my car. As I got out, I looked up at the house. It was a small, older home sitting on a hill. There were concrete steps with an iron handrail leading up to the long front porch. As I stood there I had a look on my face as though not knowing why I was there. A lady walked out from behind the house and came about half way through the front yard. It was my former pastor.

"Jane?" I whispered as she looked at me. "What's going on?"

She looked right into my eyes as she walked toward me. "I'm sorry, Mandy. I'm sorry for the pain and any actions that may have caused a set-back in your walk before God."

"I'm sorry too," I said. I honestly did not know of anything I had done, but in this dream it was crucial that I make sure everything was in the open. I started up the steps toward her, and she began to back away slowly. "Jane, why are you leaving?"

As she continued backing away, I could see a tear on her cheek. She shook her head slightly as though to indicate she was not ready for anything more at this stage, so I stopped. At that moment, the presence of God's love totally filled my being, and I could feel my heart pounding. I stood there longing to talk, but she backed away and disappeared behind the house, and I awakened.

I sat up in the bed, in disbelief. "Lord, why did I dream this?" A little later in the morning, I grabbed my things and headed out the door for work, and she came to my mind again. "Lord, why do I keep thinking about Jane?" All day at work, I had her on my mind. I came home that evening and shared my dream with my husband, who immediately suggested I try getting in touch with her. But how would I reach her? She lived in another state, and I really did not know where to begin tracking her down. I called information and asked for her name in the town we had heard she moved to, but nothing was found.

I went to work the following day, still with this on my mind. I prayed and asked God to please allow me to get in touch with her. At that point, I wanted to talk and see if we could say, "I'm sorry for *whatever* – let's go on in God."

The following morning as I was closing my front door heading out to work, the phone rang. I ran back into the kitchen to answer it and will never forget the conversation that took place. The lady on the other end of the phone was a dear sister in Christ that went to *that church* with us. We talked for a few moments and then she said, "I thought you would probably want to know this. I received a call from Brother Rick this morning and found out Jane is in the hospital with terminal breast cancer."

"What?" I nearly passed out. "Can I call her?"

"No honey, she is in the final stage. She would not allow Rick to call anyone any earlier; so no one knew of her condition until now. It's a sad thing, but all you can do is pray. I just thought you would want to know."

The feeling that swept over me was indescribable. As I hung the phone up that morning I asked, "Jesus, how could this be? Why would you let me dream a dream where she is talking and we are making everything right, and then this happen? We can now never reconcile!"

That night, I went to bed and dreamed the same dream again. Only this time, as I approached the house and began walking up the concrete steps, Jane came closer to me. "I'm sorry for all the pain I have caused. Can you please forgive me?"

"Forgive you!" I exclaimed as I took a few more steps toward her. "I love you. I too am sorry things had to end like they did. I don't want any hurt or bitterness to cause either of us our relationship with the Lord any longer. I forgive you – and ask that you forgive me too."

Then, once again she began backing up. "It's okay. It's all under the blood." As she said this, she smiled, and again, I saw a tear on her face as she vanished behind the house.

"Yes, it's under His blood." I stated, as I too wiped a tear away and turned to go toward the car. Again, I woke up and sat up in bed with my heart pounding. Staring into space, I suddenly felt God speak to my heart and tell me everything was okay.

"Lord," I said. "But I never got to talk to her."

"I made a way." I felt Him say. I then knew this was a divine dream sent from God to bring reconciliation and forgiveness. Although I never physically got to speak to my former

FROM **HURT** TO **HEALING**

STUDY GUIDE

~ *Chapter 6* ~

GO! WITH CARE
(God's Greatest Mandate . . . LOVE Unconditionally)

LOVE: A meek and gentle action, yet a mighty force; God-inspired . . . that's who He is!

01) Why is it so hard to truly love others?

(Think for a moment of that one you have a tough time loving. Is it a nosey neighbor or a complacent co-worker? Perhaps even a family member who knows how to effectively pull your chain. Could it be someone in church?)

02) How would Christ love that one (or more) named above?

03) Do you find yourself pulling away from others for fear of being hurt?

Is it difficult for you to reach out and show affection?
Have you ever been rejected when you tried?
How did you react?
What have you done since that time to overcome the fear of rejection?

No hurt cuts quite like the wound of rejection. Why is it that rejection grips so deeply within us, leaving a vacuum or hole that seems to never completely heal?

We must remember, we are made in God's own image – and what is God made of? Love! Therefore, that means above all else, we are made to love. What is the exact opposite of love? Rejection!

So, if you reach out with that very essence of what you are made of, love, and someone opposes or refuses to accept it, they are totally going against that which God naturally placed within you to give away unconditionally. That, my friend, equals a deep sense of loss – that is what you experience when you experience rejection. Know that feeling a deep hurt from being rejected is a normal way to feel. But, also know you cannot stay in the valley of rejection.

04) What can you do to counteract the deep wound rejection has left? How can you turn it around so it does not devastate your walk with God?

Stay in the arms of your First Love; The Shelter of the Almighty. Give God your highest praise in the worst of storms and watch the peace that surpasses all under-standing calm your troubled soul. Always remember, anyone can serve God when life is all sunshine and bliss. But God is looking for the heart that will say, as Job said, "Though He slay me; yet will I trust Him" (Job 13:15). That is a warrior who truly knows his Commander-in-chief. Your

Chapter 7

ENTER IN

Transformation: To change the outward form or appearance of. To change in character or condition. To cause to undergo genetic transformation (Dictionary by Merriam-Webster 2017).

Wow . . . transformation, what a glorious word. This definition describes exactly what God longs to do for *all* His children. Yes, transformation takes place when you accept Him as Savior. But so many people have bought into the lie of Satan that it ends there. You're saved from hell, so now enjoy what you can in life, muddle through any hell-on-earth that comes your way, knowing one day you will meet Jesus face-to-face and live a glorious, victorious life walking on streets of gold.

Is that the life you long for? That is not transformation. That is a butterfly stuck in its cocoon. Transformation began with salvation, but it *doesn't end there.* If you saw a little butterfly stuck in its cocoon wouldn't you think, *My goodness, will someone please teach him how to press through and live? He is in the middle of a complete transformation!* If the little butterfly does not realize who he is becoming, he may give up, never experiencing the beauty of all that was fashioned for his life.

That is what this book has been designed to do, to help those who have experienced the transformation of salvation, but found themselves stuck in deliverance's cocoon. I pray those who have been crippled by hell's deception, making them feel as though they cannot go on, are now feeling the sweet salve of the Holy Spirit ministering inner healing. And I pray your spirit has awakened, and you're screaming, "I *knew* there was *more*. Lord, I want it all!"

It's yours. God's glorious transformation is yours. The change of a life of sin, death, and defeat into a beautiful new creation, filled with purpose and expectancy is now who you are. Jeremiah 29:11 says, "For I know the thoughts that I think toward you, says the Lord, thoughts of peace and not of evil, to give you a future and a hope."

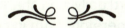

You are not asking too much when you ask God to totally transform you and radically bless your life with every good thing. It is His desire to give you the Kingdom (Luke 12:32).

You are not asking too much when you ask God to totally transform you and radically bless your life with every good thing. It is His desire to give you the Kingdom (Luke 12:32). That is the zoë life, living as kingdom people, while still here on earth. You begin by learning to overcome hurt and walk in the complete healing God has for you. Once you have done this, you will experience a more intimate relationship with your Heavenly Father than ever before. You will find yourself so in love with Jesus you will suddenly love His Word, His House, and His people more than ever before. Soon you will say, "Lord, is there more?"

The answer is a resounding, "Yes!" After accepting God's inner-healing in my life, the Lord presented a challenge. He asked something that is nothing new in His Kingdom but almost unheard of in the world in which we live.

He asked, "Will you be one of My covenant people?"

I answered, "Lord, I already am. I attend Your House every week, read Your Word daily, and share Your goodness with others. I love You, therefore I am in covenant with You."

"Your heart is earnest." The Lord spoke. "And now, if you will allow Me, I will teach you how to become one of My covenant people."

"Yes Lord, I accept the challenge. Teach me what it means to be forever in covenant with You."

"Begin by reading the book of Deuteronomy." As the Lord instructed, I opened His Word to Deuteronomy and quickly informed Him I had already read most of it while attending a school of ministry. (As though He wasn't aware of that.)

However, I did not realize that I did not yet fully understand what it meant to be in covenant with my Savior, *but God did.*

As His children, we accept His everlasting covenant of salvation when we ask Him to be Lord of our lives. That is His wonderful, miraculous covenant called grace, given to us when we, by faith, accept Him as Lord. But there is a realm to this covenant that extends far beyond the boundaries of salvation. It was never intended to be a mystery. God's Word has always openly displayed this supernatural God-given, grace-filled, and overwhelmingly unexplainable love covenant awaiting us. We had just never pressed into that place in Him to see its fullness.

God's true covenant is what He is—Love. Pure, undefiled, and open to all. And that, Beloved, is who we are reborn to be!

Are you willing to accept the Father's challenge and enter into this Covenant of Love? If yes, please open your Bible to Deuteronomy, bow your head, and in your own way tell your Heavenly Father that you desire to be included as one of His covenant people. Ask Him to open unto you His full revelation of the life of covenant, as He intended it.

After accepting the challenge and reading the book of Deuteronomy, there is one last passage you must see, so you may fully understand all Christ is saying. Go now to Hebrews and read chapters 11 and 12. You will recognize chapter eleven. It is what we modern-day Christians refer to as the "Hall of Faith." However, you must not stop there.

Read through chapter 12 to get a complete understanding of what God is saying regarding covenant.

Upon reading the above referenced passages, the Lord brought fresh revelation, and I saw covenant in a greater light than ever before. I'd like to share that word with you. Please read with an open heart and His open Word. Don't take just my words for it – let scripture speak for itself.

~⚹ ⚹~

The Deuteronomy Covenant People
Vs.
The Hebrews Covenant "By Faith" People

Reading through the pages of Deuteronomy, you are acquainted with God's people whom He intended to be His covenant people. You see the deliverance, the miraculous, the rebellion and the blessing.

God loved His people just as much when they were in Egypt as He did when they came out of Egypt. He loved them just as much when they were encamped in the wilderness as He did when they entered into the Promised Land.

So, what's the difference?

Those who loved their God enough to become a covenant people, came into total agreement with His Love, and He was, therefore, able to give the fullness of His love unto them. He never loved those in Egypt less than those in the wilderness, nor those in the wilderness less than those in the Promised Land . . .

But here is the difference:

Have you ever loved someone with everything you had to give but they did not reciprocate that love, or love you back in the same measure? Picture this. You love your church and your pastor. You know you are in the house, or vineyard, God has placed you in to work for Him, and you want to be able to show your love and faithfulness.

Imagine you are standing now in front of your pastor, and there is one other person standing to your right who is fairly new to the congregation. She doesn't know your pastor's heart or the heart of the ministry as you do, and she, too, is facing you.

As you look into your pastor's face with great love from your Heavenly Father you say, "I love you. I love this ministry, and I pray nothing ever separates us." As you are expressing your love, suddenly, the other person steps in between you and your pastor. She begins asking questions about many things within the church. They seem like valid questions. She continues on, one comment after the other, until finally, you're trying to tell your pastor, "I love you and am committed to you," but you start to feel confused. What *if* something *is* wrong within the church? Your pastor is still standing, unmoved before God, yet you feel a wedge between you like never before—what is happening?

You have not entered into covenant with your pastor, or the ministry you are presently serving in. Yes, you may have signed a membership roll, but your heart is torn. You want to love. You truly do, but you are now looking around and questioning things and wondering if everything is true and real.

We do this same thing with God. Just as the children of Israel did. I can just imagine God standing before them with His arms extended wide, indulging in a conversation that might go something like this: "You are my people. I love you and I want to give you everything. I have a land flowing with milk and honey that awaits you; a land in which you will never lack for anything again. Receive my love."

Imagine those who might answer "Yes Lord, I receive," opening their arms and locking their arms in the arms of God, thus, sealing their covenant. Heaven would meet earth, and nothing, absolutely nothing, could come between that child of God and his or her Heavenly Father.

Go back to the scene previously portrayed. How would the scene differ when you have come into covenant with your pastor and your church?

You are standing in front of your pastor. There is a person to your right, questioning many things going on. You hear her concerns, but you are not affected. Why? Look at the scene. You have walked up, opened your arms, and interlocked arms with your pastor. Arm to arm, heart to heart, and spirit to spirit. When arms and spirits are locked, nothing is allowed in between them. There is no open space for the enemy – a covenant is sealed.

God so loved His people that He wanted to give them His *all*. Yet, it was only possible with those who would come into covenant with Him, interlocked so nothing (not fear, doubt, unbelief, offense, or other tactics of hell) could come between them.

So, what about the others? Those who did not love Him enough to come into covenant, died in Egypt or in the wilderness. But covenant people entered the Promised Land!

There were three groups of people included within the children of Israel, and those groups are still relevant for the children of God today:

First: The Egyptians

Some of God's people never left Egypt. They may have physically come out of Egypt, but they never "left" Egypt. (Where your heart is, there will your treasure be also.) Egypt was all they thought about. How can you know?

Because whenever something hard came up, challenging them, what was the first thing to come out of their mouth? "We would have been better off to have stayed in Egypt." They constantly referred back to that place from which they had been delivered . . . in their heart, they never really left! They were not covenant people; they were Egyptians.

Second: The Wanderers

They wanted more than what Egypt offered, but they just weren't sure about those "covenant people." They took things way too seriously. I mean, yeah Egypt was bad, but do we *really* want to do things totally different? Is that really necessary? Hey, there may have been a few good things back there. So, should I go, should I not, should I look back, should I move forward? Do Moses and Aaron, and Joshua and Caleb (the leaders) really even know what they're doing? They've admitted this is a brand-new thing for them. No one's ever traveled here before. Should I follow them? I wonder, and I wander, and that's exactly what they did, for *forty years.* Constantly pulled between Egypt and the Promised Land.

They were not covenant people; they were Wanderers.

Third: Who Were These Odd People?

These were those who did not look back and long for the things of the past (the good, the bad, or the ugly). They did not wonder nor wander, nor have any desire to go through the struggles and turmoil they had seen their parents, and even themselves perhaps, endure. They looked ahead to what was to come and there were no rearview mirrors.

They did not flinch, although at times their hearts would break for the Egyptians and the Wanderers because they loved them, but they loved their God more! So, they embraced this new thing, this new place God was taking them. They continued on, in spite of all odds, all battles, turmoil, and distraction – and they did what no others before them had ever done – they reached out to this God of Love and locked arms (heart, mind, spirit, and soul) with His and came into covenant.

They allowed Him to give His *all*, and He gave unto them the Promised Land; a new way of life, flowing with milk and honey (fullness abounding). The very best, of the very best.

These *were* the Covenant People!

So, what about those that thought it was too much to ask? They still got to see the miraculous things that God did. I mean, He did some pretty awesome things in the wilderness. They didn't miss out on *seeing the miraculous*. They missed out on *living the miraculous*!

Have you witnessed God do some pretty awesome things? Have you seen lives transformed, healings manifest, and listened to overcoming testimonies of miraculous proportion? You have now come too far–you know too much–to be allowed to remain neutral before God.

Look one last time at the Deuteronomy covenant people. Look back at the Hebrews "By Faith" covenant people. You now have a choice to make.

Will you accept the challenge? Will you reach out and embrace God's covenant of love? Will you lock arms – heart, mind, soul, and spirit – with your Heavenly Father, and with those He has called you to serve Him in covenant with?

You *are* one of the three:

An "Egyptian," always looking back;

A "Wondering Wanderer," always questioning and living in confusion;–or -

ENTER IN

A Covenant Keeper, accepting God's total love and direction, unconditionally.

God will love you the very same regardless of your decision, but choosing anything less than covenant means missing out on *all* that could have been yours while here on earth.

Will you embrace His love, and all He has called you to? Will you lock arms in covenant?

The choice is yours.

You were created in the image of God, the Creator of the universe, and worlds without end. This God, full of love, is also your loving Heavenly Father. You are His child; a Kingdom kid.

There is great destiny within you, for Heaven's DNA flows through your veins. You were created by love, to be love. Hurt was never God's way.

My prayer, as you have read through the pages of this book, is:

- That you now see yourself through God's eyes and are captivated by His love *for* you and His purpose *within* you.

- That you determine hurt will no longer define who you are, but you'll instead walk in love bringing hope to the hurting.

- That you will be that covenant person God created you to be, locking arms with your Heavenly Father and fellowship of believers He has planted you with.

May you step from wandering in the wilderness into the fullness of destiny God has designed and appointed for you as you now journey, from hurt to healing, all for the glory of God!

AUTHOR BIO

❦

M andy Pierce resides in the Sevier County, Tennessee area with her husband, Tom. They have two grown sons, T.J. (and wife Katie) and Caleb (and wife Ali).

Tom and Mandy have worked in children's ministry over thirty years, teaching in the local church as well as at a national youth camp.

They have recently entered the world of foster parenting, and feel honored God is allowing them to work with children needing a safe refuge while in search of a forever home.

Reference List

Bible Study Tools. "Zoe—New Testament Greek Lexicon—King James Version." n.d. Accessed June 10, 2019. https://www.biblestudytools.com/lexicons/greek/kjv/zoe.html.

Dictionary by Merriam-Webster: America's Most-trusted Online Dictionary. "Definition of TRANSFORMED." n.d. Accessed June 14, 2019. https://www.merriam-webster.com/dictionary/transformed.

Genetic Science Learning Center. "Extra or Missing Chromosomes." Learn.Genetics. February 15, 2014. Accessed June 13, 2019. https://learn.genetics.utah.edu/content/disorders/extraormissing/.

Lexico Dictionaries | English. "Genesis | Definition of Genesis in English by Lexico Dictionaries." n.d. Accessed June 14, 2019. https://www.lexico.com/en/definition/genesis.

Lexico Dictionaries | English. "Genetic | Definition of Genetic in English by Lexico Dictionaries." n.d. Accessed June 14, 2019. https://www.lexico.com/en/definition/genetic.

Lexico Dictionaries | English. "Heredity | Definition of Heredity in English by Lexico Dictionaries." n.d.

Accessed June 14, 2019. https://www.lexico.com/en/ definition/heredity.

Swindoll, Charles R. *Strengthening Your Grip: How to be Grounded in a Chaotic World.* Worthy Books, 1982.

Zodhiates, Spiros. *The Hebrew-Greek Key Word Study Bible: King James Version.* Edited by Warren Baker. Chatanooga TN: AMG Pubs, 1991.

CPSIA information can be obtained
at www.ICGtesting.com
Printed in the USA
LVHW030511201119
637929LV00004B/4/P

9 781545 678718